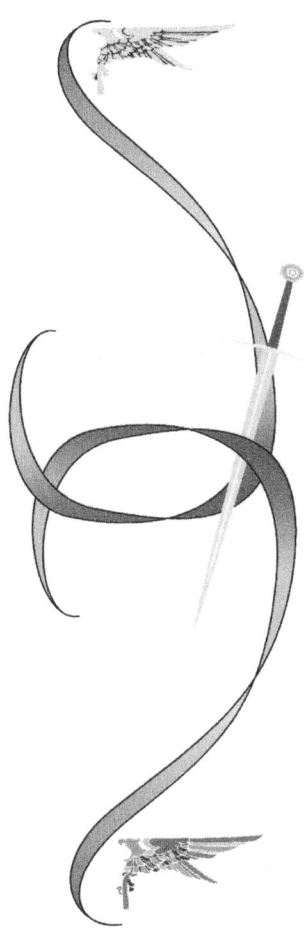

Intimate Relationship with Jesus

© Copyright Sheri Hauser 2020
Published by Glorybound Publishing
SAN 256-4564
Printed in the United States of America
3rd Edition
KDP ISBN 9798580632636
Copyright data available on file.
Hauser, Sheri, 1957-
     Intimate Relationship with Jesus/Sheri Hauser
     Includes biographical reference.
1. Ancient Mysteries   2. Charismatic interest/Prophecy.   I. Title

www.gloryboundpublishing.com

The cover image is used from Hubble NASA.

Intimate Relationship with Jesus

My Pillow Talk

by Sheri Hauser

Glorybound Publishing
Camp Verde, Arizona, USA
in the year 2020

Introduction

This book came about when another book, originally entitled *Miracle's* was split in half like a piece of paper on edge. In order to understand what Pillow Talk is about, it is important to recognize its history. When I first began writing, as reviewed in the Letter from the Author which follows, I was drawn by the Holy Spirit and issued a personal challenge to God asking Him to teach me to love Him the in a different way. I had grown weary of attempting to be 'spiritual' by learning Church programs, attending Bible College and memorizing volumes of Scripture.

At the age of 40, I was a 'washed out' Christian with a feeling that Christianity didn't really work for those who had real problems. Being faced with a troubled marriage, financial problems and distressed teens, I was at the end of my rope feeling abandoned by the religion which I had put my hope into for many years.

It was at this point that I issued a challenge to God. Indeed, it was bold to assume I could speak to the Creator of the Universe with such a casual tone, but I felt that, being overwhelmed with such exasperation, I was in a special situation and, if He was who He said He was, then He would be gracious and give a little mercy.

God met my challenge by sending the Holy Spirit. I opened my life in a new way to become a place where He took control. My challenge was easy, "If You are who You say (through the Bible) You are, then enter into me as it is written in John 14 and teach me how to love You."

The first book I wrote was a composite of poetry and dreams. The subject was based on the book of Proverbs recognizing that God's wisdom is greater than ours. We don't really know who we are except that we can ask our parents and friends, and then combine with education to come out with a result. But, what if we were to ask God, and learn to listen to His response? Surely the One who created us knows the original intention of our lives better than anyone else.

That first book was quite lengthy and combined refreshing love poetry with dogmatic instruction related to how God speaks today. Being instructed by God in dreams not to release any of the books, I continued to write and, before I knew it, I had four books completed: Miracule's, Tomaseña, Katísha and Coríanta.

Inclined to be grateful for the outpouring which had been given to me, I prayed and decided to give my first fruit book to God as an offering.

In essence, I laid the first-born, *Miracle's* on the altar and returned it to God. When I did, He kept it. That first book as it was originally written, will never be published. As soon as I 'gave' the book to Him, He began giving a series of dreams changing the manuscript and re-directing the outcome of the original book to such a degree that I was inclined to set several pieces aside as the book was redesigned.

The second version of *Miracule's* includes 7 Holy books and is intended to include those of all religious preferences. Therefore all of the pieces which were not 'generically inclined' were set aside. In 2008 the second version of *Miracule's* was published. At that point, I sized up the stack of writings which I had set aside based on the parameters of the book I was given in dreams and discovered they added up to another book!

Intimate Relationship with Jesus is the other side of the piece of paper from the split of the original manuscript called *Miracle's*. The book is mushy and paints a picture of a woman swooned by a lover, the Holy Spirit. Enjoy my soap opera for I have been cleansed by the blood of the Lamb and fallen in love with my Jesus.

Letter from the Author

In 2001 I received a dream. Then I had it again. When it came to me the third time, I took notice of it. I couldn't help but to think of Moses stopping to notice the bush on fire wondering why it wasn't consumed. I wondered why this dream wasn't consumed by time. Why didn't it pass like all the others?

And, like Moses, when I paused, I found something greater than what looked to be ordinary. I took the dream to God in my prayer time and asked Him for the answer to it. How amazing! He responded with another dream. I was awe struck to recognize that my questions were responded to like a volley ball in a game: He sent the answer back to me in a dream again and again.

At first, I was shocked and kept the information to my self and then I shared with a few close friends. Some admonished me to 'put away the foolishness' while others pacified me, tossing my 'interpretations of dreams' into waste cans when they felt I wasn't looking. But, they kept coming and like a 'secret rendezvous each night, I set a notebook with a pen by my bedside eager for another 'encounter' with my new friend 'the voice that responds back in dreams'. Certainly, it had to be God because He was the one I was asking for answers. Who else knows the answers?

And, I fell in love. I couldn't help it. When the dream came:

'I am looking for night dreamers to become day doers who do what I only dreamt of until I found you.'

That sounded like a personal letter from God to me. I became addicted to understanding the dreams because they were like 'post-its' from God.

So, I copied the dreams down in the middle of the night onto a pad and used Scripture and prayer to understand them as signs from God. It was an amazing development just like getting the lid off a can of beans. Once the lid is off, you can eat all the beans you want. Once the lid was off the idea that dreams came to me as 'messages from God in response to prayers' I consumed all I could at an alarming rate.

I began putting the dreams into the computer because my handwriting was illegible from being transcribed onto my notebook in the middle of the night. I was at this stage after about a year from receiving the first dream [several times] when I received another significant dream. In this dream there were just words in which God said, "You are writing a book".

Now, I'm not a writer, by trade. I am a nurse. And, I have never attempted to write anything other than term papers, so I am confident that, if God wanted me to 'write a book' it was supposed to be compilation of these files of dreams. At that point I had no idea of the topic. To me, the dreams had come as answers to my prayers, leading for my life, and words of caution which steered me away from things that would potentially harm me.

So, I decided to pile up the dreams three times. I figured that, with the chances of odds, I could be able to come up with a reliable pattern by the third try. Well, I piled them up two times after about six months. But, the problems was that while I was attempting to 'arrange my pile' I was being overwhelmed by more and more dreams; sometimes as many as four a night.

One of the things that I do, when I can't figure out what else to do, is to fast. So, I fasted because I was urgent to know the answer of how this pile of dreams came together. After a forty day fast, God gave me a dream which led me to an outline for all of the dreams. It was Isaiah 11.2-3. So, I compiled all of the dreams with their 'interpretations' into one book. It was five hundred notebook pages. {To help you understand, this is about 1500 pages in a regular size book.} During this time I started receiving 'words' which came like 'poetry', as well. I didn't know what to do with these 'words', so I put them in a separate file and called them 'Reflections of Praise'.

The night I completed the book, I handed it to God and considered myself 'done' with the project. But, that night He gave me 4 dreams. In those dreams He told me to set the book on my dresser for forty nights whereby He would give instructions over that time. He likened it to Noah and the Ark. Noah took 100 years to build the Ark, then God closed him up in the boat for a few days before it rained. I bet those 7 days while they waited for it to rain were tough on Noah because I can imagine that he got taunting from the nearby people and, probably, even his family. And, God showed me that, like Noah, I had taken 40 years to complete a project which should have been done a long time ago, I needed to be patient and given Him a few days to work out the details.

Over the next 40 days, He gave me dreams which directed me to 'chop' up that book into four books. Then, He told me to 'turn the stack over and release them. Well, the dreams kept coming at an alarming rate and hearing the voice of God pushed into the daytime. What happened was that the books 'exploded' in the center. The first book kept being pushed further and further back while others were inserted.

At this point I have completed 19 books and am, finally, ready to compile Pillow Time which is the other side of Miracule's. To me, this is the first book which I wrote, so I am happy to finally be releasing it. Sheri.....

It is now 2020 and I am re-releasing newer versions of the same books. The amazing thing is that the first one re-released is the first one that I originally wrote. I changed the title so that people will understand what the book is about and put an amazing picture on the cover which speaks of the mystical nature of God. I am doing the same with this book, originally entitled Pillow Talk--and now entitled Intimate Relationship with Jesus. What I (finally) saw was that the books came to me one way and need to be released to others a different way. What came to me as Pillow Talk (with Jesus), now comes to you as **Intimate Relationship with Jesus**. I sincerely hope it blesses your soul and encourages you to find your own pillow talk with Him.

Dream Cachë

Welcome to Sheri's dream cache releasing what has been kept hidden until now. There are stores of riches kept in a vault up to this day, which open the door of understanding the voice of God in dreams as answers to prayer. The wind, the storm, the rain and the lightening of God is coming. Feel the wind? There is always a gentle breeze just before the tornado. Oh how we have looked for the eye of the storm in this world in which we live, yet we have not found it. We have prayed, yet we are not healed. We have spent countless hours on our knees without finding our deliverance. Our children remain on drugs; our families are still in bondage; we are yet poor and destitute. Our Churches are poor, filled with empty pews and singers off cue. Where are the answers to our prayers? We have been tricked by our enemies. They have snuck in and left seeds of doubt which grew into a cancer eating away at our faith in God. Our vision has been clouded by our own sinfulness and lust for the things of this world. Yet we continue to seek for a force outside ©ourselves which will save us from this dreadful condition which we are in. Where is He? Take encouragement, friends, I have brought a fresh shipment of hope: It's the hope of hearing the voice of God for yourself. Just like Moses heard the voice of the Lord and brought Salvation to the Children of Israel, He is bringing the same today. Has God changed? No. Suppose you ask a question in prayer: Do you expect an answer? There is one, you know? I am here to help you reach out to God in a special way and enable the enemies of doubt within your life to be crushed and conquered. What I bring is a bridge to faith. We attempt to reach a God we do not know; only have heard about from those going on before us. But, when we reach into that darkness, we are unsure of a connection: Will there be a hand reaching back to us? We don't really know. That is faith, my friend. Faith reaches into the unknown seeking something you are unsure of while trusting that there will be an answer on the other side. Welcome to my dream Cachë. It is like a jewelry box filled with gems, sparkling in the moonlight: dreams that come to life as the voice of God dances through my head night after night. And, He wants the same for you. He told me, so. Your dreams and visions can be a bridge to a relationship with God giving encouragement, hope, help, and direction hidden in this vault of wondrous pictures sent straight from heaven. I have propped open for you five doors and a window . I encourage you to learn to seek God through learning to understand His voice as it comes to you His way, now as you are comfortable accepting it. Remember, God came in thunder, storm and a wind in times before. Why wouldn't He now? May I present this shipment of Grace. For it is by the Grace of God that we are saved. Remember that.

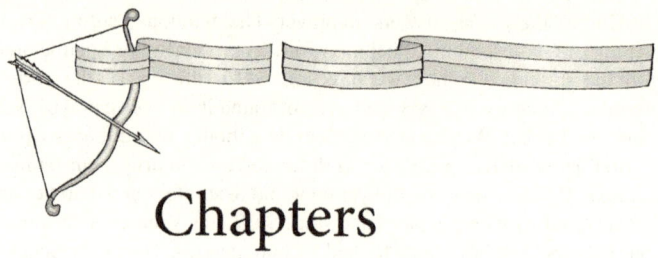

Chapters

1. Hungry Heart
2. Indwelling
3. Rainbow of His Love
4. The Dance
5. John 14-16 Merge
6. Growing Service
7. Seal of Zeal

About the Author- 241

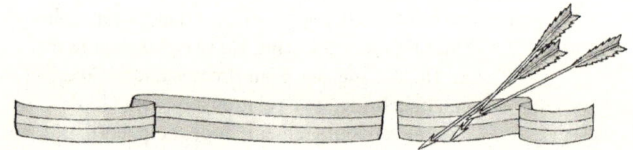

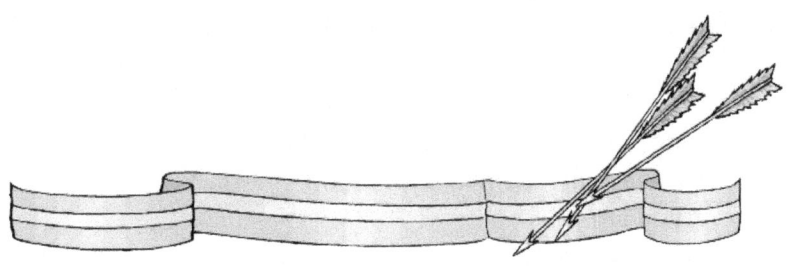

Chapter I
Hungry Heart

The Conquesta: Healing of the Nations

Agony and desperation, desire and longing,
hungry and lacking, like a sick coyote near the road we cry out.
Sacrifice is the solution. Not ours, but His.
We never saved anybody. We just glean the fields.
Pick up what He plants.
Invite the family. It's the season to work together
for the healing of the nations. Foreign to foreigners.
We give them God's message from Heaven.
We don't have to understand them.
He does. Jesus goes in front of us preparing the way room by room.

He moves through conquesta matadore temporteria de almandero.
(transported to the majesty of the conquest){Tongues}

White Gloves of Justification

Where's the justification for your sin?
Your hands are stained with blood.
For you are
sinners and cannot redeem yourselves.
Put on the white gloves that I hold out
to you with My own hands.
Be covered, be free, become,
cleansed, redeemed, justified.

Love Note

Written on a piece of the worst paper
possible. A tree. It's a favorite old love
song.
How He died for me.
He didn't chose onion paper.
He didn't choose stationery.
He didn't use a note pad
and He doesn't have
a typewriter.
But He
used a
human
heart
to
write His
love note on.
A heart of gold.

Jesus Is

Jesus is the life blood given
for your sins.
His life for us.
His blood for ours,
To give us life through it.

Redemption Letters

Stealing alphabet soup from a child.
Letters have been taken from
His Son that spell redemption.

Love of the Father

Actually, it was the Father that has protected us
from the wrath of judgment from the Son.
It is He who judges the world.
The Father sent the Son.

Savior Parfait

Blessed redemption brought by a Virgin!
Delight to our soul, pure and holy, love and joy!
Savior Parfait.
Morning Delight!

Three Scoops of Love

In love
once, twice, thrice.
We were his first love, and
still are. What precious love, what
riches for us to enjoy. Like three
scoops in one ice cream
cone. It's a sugar
cone with a triple
dip of His love.
Hold on tight.

Meet at the Altar

Desire and longing meet anticipation and joy at the altar.

Hungry

Hungry?
Come to the
table of the King.
He will provide for you.
He has food from a King to a daughter.
It is all that he wants to provide for His Church.

Jesus Fanatic Diet

Diets are for losers to loose what they don't want to keep.
Loose your weights and sins.
Drop them at the foot of Jesus.
Become light.
It's a Jesus Fanatic diet.

Seven Heart Tones of God

The colors of God are reflected in the Holy Spirit.
Beautiful tones of His heart.

For, when you put your ear to His chest, and listen to His heart beat, there is more than just lub-dub, like us. You know, we have two tones that are echoed when the valves of our heart open and close. They reflect the action of the pump within the center of our chest. If we listen with a stethoscope we can hear the heart. A cardiologist can tell if the heart is normal simply by listening because his ear has been trained to discern the different heart tones. The sounds are made by the movement of the mechanics of the muscle as it thrusts blood to the rest of the body. If it doesn't sound right, then there is an indication that there is a problem with the flow of the blood to the body.

The heart of God has 7 tones. Presence, Fear of the Lord, Wisdom, Might, Knowledge, Understanding, and Council. Each of these are like valves where the blood of Jesus flows to His body, the church. Each valve has a specific tone that correlates with the action of that evidence of the function of God. They are all outlets of His grace and Mercy, His love and healing, His deliverance and Salvation, His kindness and power.

None is more important than the other, for they all are part of His heart. They are the center of who He is, the love muscle of Almighty God.

When we come to God through the blood of Jesus, it is like entering into His blood stream. He opens the way and puts us into the arteries of God. Are free to float within the blood stream by the power of the Holy Spirit and enter through the many heart valves of God. They become gateways to one another. There are interrelationships between the heart valves of God, just as there are relationships between our valves.

Our goal is to recognize God's heart in things and hear those tones. Only when our ear is on His chest, can we hear his heart beat. The issue that we must continue to resolve is where is our ear? Are we listening to our own heart, the heart of others, or God's heart?

For us to desire some of His tones with disregard for the others does not honor Him. He has made all of the valves to be used to move the blood of Jesus through the body, the Church, to bring about His purposes.

There is an avenue of flow as it moves through the heart of God. The Fear of the Lord invites Him, even when we are afraid of Him. As we invite Him, He comes. His presence races to us. We continue to get to know Him, and He shares His mind with us. He tells us his plans in the valve of Council. He shares his desires with the valve of wisdom. He brings us understanding in that we could never relate to a divine being from earth without His interpretation of it for us. Then, He brings it all together with the valve of Might. The valve of Might is like the Aortic Valve. It is the one that pushes the flow to the rest of the body. Might is the added power to prove that He is God. For, only God would have the ability to push His Word throughout the whole body of Christ.

****

The Dam Broke

The dam broke when Jesus died.
His blood flowed down to all below and
still does. They never fixed that dam.
Nobody has the power except Him
and He does not want it fixed.
He likes it broken. He broke it
on purpose to send some stuff
down stream to the thirsty,
hungry and lonely
people
down
stream
so they
could drink
of
His tide, eat of Him
an be healed. It took more
power to break it than to sustain it.

Love to a Little Girl

The Dream
I am snuggling with my husband. There were two other guys in the room. Everybody knows each other well and enjoy spending time together, snuggling like kittens caressing one another.

Then a 3 year old came into the room. Paul becomes the father and there is a mother as well.

She says, "Daddy, my butt is sore." They went trail riding in the morning.

Then she looks at me and says, "My Daddy loves me no matter what I do. My Daddy will always love me. He loves his little girl."

Second dream:
I look in the mirror and my eyes are beautiful. Beautiful green, just like the little girl. I am the little girl.

Interpretation:
These are all pictures of who God wants to be to me. He wants to snuggle with me, just like my husband. He is telling me that all of the three, Father, Son and Holy Spirit enjoy being close to me. It is amazing that they are so incredibly personal with one another and with me. They want me to be as personal with them as they are with one another.

He is like my mother and my father all at once. He trains and instructs. He teaches, then shows me the way to go. It is similar to a father taking his daughter on trail rides. He is in front of me always. Sometimes the ride is bumpy. He knows that I am low on endurance, like a small child. He understands.

But I have come to understand him, too. I understand his love to me. He knows that I am not afraid to tell others. He has given me calm assurance. I know that he loves me no matter what I do. He likes to take me trail riding, but he understands that I may get tired. He still loves me even when I am not doing all he has told me to do. He will always love me. It is an eternal relationship. He loves his little girl.

My eyes reflect to others that love of God to me. And that is all I need to do. Go ahead and look at them. They see it.

Deuteronomy 30.20, Joshua 22.5, Psalms 31.23, 87.2, Proverbs 22.11, 29.3, Isaiah 43.4, 63.9, Jeremiah 31.3, Hosea 3.1, 11.4, Zephaniah 3.17, John 13.34, 14.21, 15, 17.24, Romans 8.35, I Corinthians 5.14, 6.6, Eph 2.4, 6.23, 2 Thessalonians 3.5.

At first I didn't want to put this dream into the book, but God told me to. It is because He wants to be incredibly personal with all of his children. He wants to take all of them on the trail with him. He knows how much we can endure, and is right there with us each step of the way.

This dream is one that I left all of the verses I researched to come up with the answer. I think He wanted me to show others that, even the message sounds incredibly simple, I had to work to get there. It took endurance. And, after I did, His glory is reflected in the outcome.

Two arm Rescue

To have and to hold.
Let Me have you,
I hold you,
I got you.
It's a
two arm pull to safety.
Grace
Comes
to us like a fireman
rescues someone from a mountainside.
God
grabs us with both hands as we reach out ours.
And, He   holds on.
Just like a two arm firefighter's hold. He will never
let go until we are in our father's arms safe and sound.

Geronimo

Jump
out
launch
forward,
take a leap,
step out in faith,
tests the wind, bring your gear,
wear your shoes, exercise firm footing
on target, on the cross, where you're meant to land.
If you never get out the door, you will not launch out,
you will not fly, you will never learn to soar and never
end up at the X. It marks the spot, the place where we
should all end up.
The Cross

His Son

Seated at his right-hand in Glory
Forevermore captured by His
love,
held within His hope,
between the hands
of time,
is His
glory
and
His
power
His might, His
magnificence, His Son.

The Steps

Dream:
A Christian brother and I were leading others on the path to God. There were many steps like on the way to a government building. They are small steps all leading upward. Stephanie, my daughter is very tired. She is carrying a heavy load. I carry her. We go up many steps. Then some people show up. At first we see a little robotic thing. It looks like a snowman on wheels that is remote controlled.

There is a question, "Will they rescue us maybe?"

I am very tired of carrying Stephanie.

Interpretation:
My brother and I are leading others on a path to God through a series of steps that lead to the Kingdom of God. It is similar to God's place of rule; his palace. It is his government. (Isa 11)

Stephanie, my daughter, represents the Church. The Church is the daughter of God. He is raising us to become the bride of Christ.

The Church is carrying a heavy load. Why? What is the load? Perhaps, we are carrying loads that we should put down. There are things that we ought not be packing around, that we are, thinking that we may need them. It is like taking along a back-pack with our lunch when we go to communion.

Sometimes, we they are hard to put down. Maybe, it is something that we have carried for a long time and we are used to carrying it. Perhaps we have guilt over wrongful sexual behavior when we were small children. We carry this. It is like a burden; a thing. We get used to it because we have carried it for so long.

The dream gives us the message to lay down our burdens. Nearly everyone carries anger, guilt, and some feelings of being 'wronged' in a relationship at one time. We need to let that go. Leave it at the bottom of the stairs because it will slow our walk along the path to where God wants us to be.

Other burdens are rules that we inflict on ourselves. Religious leaders encourage us to grow closer to God. As they encourage us, often then suggest ideas on how we can do this. Sometimes, however, we go overboard, and get stuck on the rules instead of the purpose for them. We need to be careful that rules of service are not laying burdens on our brothers and sisters rather than freeing them, the way that we intend them to.

The remote controlled snowman is something that is controlled by someone else in a different location. It is built by a man to resemble a snowman, but it can be moved at the discretion of the controller. It is mechanical. (If you haven't guessed.) It is the presentation of redemption through Jesus' blood in a mechanical form. Isaiah 1.18 relates redemption to snow. It says that though our sins be as scarlet they will be white as snow, though they be red and crimson, they will be white as wool. Jesus came to wash us like snow.

The robotics snowman symbolizes the things that come between us within the body of Christ and may cause us to trip on the stairs. It is not controlled by God, but by men. It is offering the forgiveness of Jesus robotically, to others. It causes God to be 'remote' from the individual. It is mechanical redemption. Mechanical prayer.

In the dream, I carry my daughter. We, as the Children of God, carry the Church. We carry it as a banner. It is ours. We bear it because it has been born from us. It is us. And, even though, it has issues; burdens; we still carry it. We still love it.

The question that is asked on the stairs is, "Will they rescue us?"

The situation is that the Church is overburdened with tradition and religion. Then, there is a problem of God being 'remote' because of us being robotic as we invite God to be part of our lives. We are deep in a path of 'cook book' evangelism, disciple programs, and seminaries. These are robotics and remote. They seek to control the sheep rather than feed them.

In the last scene of the dream a question is asked. There is a question as to whether those on the stair were sent to help direct us to God. So, I asked this question to God, "Who did You send to help me find You?"

The answer I received was that He has given us the Holy Spirit to help direct us in the steps toward His Holy Kingdom. The Holy Spirit is represented by more than one person, because He manifests Himself in several ways, and sometimes we see Him differently. He is not a different person, but sometimes we see Him from the side, and other times from the front. He shows us which ever profile we need at that time.

Psalms 68.19, Isaiah 1.18, 11, Matthew 11.30, Luke 11.46, Galatians 6.2.

Ability

I know He has given us the ability to find Him.
Share it, declare it, uphold it, envision it.

Complicate Simplicity

Wonderful Lord, Savior complete.
Why do I addd to what He has done for me?
I complicate simplicity.

Coordinated Victory

It is a coordinated effort between the Father,
the Son and the Holy Spirit
that enables us to live in the world, not be of the world,
and have victory every step
of the way. Jesus gave us new birth, it is the Father's Kingdom,
and the Holy Spirit is our counselor.

Despite it All

Despite
all odds, He came.
Despite all odds, He died.
Despite all odds, He rose again.
Despite, the spite of all, He still lives,
to love us all.

His Front Doors

He gives us more front doors.
Places to walk through.
There is no back door.

Buffalo Nickel

Does a buffalo have one hump or two?
If a buffalo could get over his hump,
I could get over you.
I love you.
Let me shoulder you like the buffalo.
You know, he's on the nickel.

Our Stand

Be sturdy, stand strong, powerful
and mighty against the foe.
For he only pretends to.
He crawls because
God
has removed
his basis for
stand.

No War in Prayer

There need not be war in prayer.
Walk to the ridge and look.
God will call down fire on them as you desire.
Go stand, turn and face what He has given you.
It's your ground. Welcome to the family.

Everything Else

What happened when Jesus died?
I'm not sure.
What happened when He rose?
Everything else.

Summer Snow

How do you get snow in the summer?
Look up   and ask.
Why   not?
Forgiveness
and
light.
Good
combination.
It's   always
the season for Jesus.

(Based on Isaiah 1:18,19)

Jesus Breaks the Seal

Jesus breaks the seal on a letter from a King.

Asleep All My Life

Help me, Jesus
For I have been asleep all my life.
Wake me to the knowledge of your presence in my soul.
Open the eyes of my heart to see what you see,

when you see it, from Your perspective.

Children Deserted Dad

Ere, you found me, I was already there.
Alas, where did you go?

Over the hill and through the bushes
Like children looking for plastic eggs
in an Easter Egg Hunt at the park.
Adventure is for the fun at heart.
What happened?
I turned around and you were gone.

It is a family park.
The children deserted dad.

Where's the children I love?
They have turned their faces to
The wind. Where did they go?
Any way, but the way I have directed.
They have shown others a luke warm view of God;
A God without power, love and ability to deliver.
They don't know Me because they are too
busy seeking their golden calf.
They have invested too much,
and they are looking for the return.

Fresh Oil

The fresh oil from the newly paved road can stick to your souls. The Holy Spirit is the oil that paves the way down the road to the Holiness of God. It is His Oil of our anointing, healing, deliverance, mercy, and grace that coat the fine rocks of the revelation of God's Word. When our road is coated with the fresh oil, it will shine, but it will be hot. Let the oil stain your shoes. Our walk carries his blood stain.
We walk in the way Jesus walked, in the Spirit.
We carry His anointing oil wherever we go.
And we track it into the house of God.
Even when we leave a place,
there remains a stain
in the carpet
where we
walked.
Others
can't
remove it.
It is the stain of the Spirit of God.
It is
like
oil based
paint, it is not easily
removed. The base is different
from those around us, for it is eternal.
And it is left within our footprints as we walk
in then Spirit of Grace, carrying the presence of God, embodied within the Holy Spirit who lives in us.

Confirmation on the Bridge

Confirmation is a step, not a process. A break
point. A place where your toes have been hanging
over the cliff, and now you step out hoping there is
a bridge that will lead to where you know He told you
to go. The deal with this bridge, though, is it's a swinging
foot bridge. Sometimes, those of us who are scared need
confirmation with each rickety board. For, when we look
over the rope handle that we cling to, And down 200 yards
into the raging river below, we have a hard time focusing
on the original goal. Sometimes, God gives us a mission
that is like a rope bridge. It spans a considerable distance
between two points that have been separated until now.
He wants to bring His presence to the other side.
And, although, He built the bridge through
sending Jesus Christ, Jesus bridges
the way to God. Although,
He built the
bridge,
He needs
someone to
walk across that flimsy mesh of twisted frayed
nylon ropes. Because, that bridge
goes to the
other side
and He needs
to bring a message
there. So, you can quit peeking
over the side, or ask for confirmation
along the way. Both, are probably a good idea.

Confirmation Bridge

Confirmation is for those who are not sure.
Faith bridges the gap between insecurity
and getting Where we need to be.
God
is always happy to confirm
His word. Don't be
afraid to ask for
confirmation.

Zeal

The big dog in the little tent has been sleeping on a shelf.
P   a   s   s   i   o   n
Has been aroused. He is awake now.
He is waking the other dogs.
Jealousy   and
Zeal for
God.

Driving Agony

Satan drives agony and despair.
Agony constricts finances.
Despair takes everything away
leaving you penniless and
desperate.

Fires of Passion and Bitterness

Revenge comes from where the fire starts.
Left unattended it will burn taking that whole
area of growth with it. Given enough time and
change of seasons, dampens the blaze, but embers
glow in the areas with the most damage. There they
burn red hot waiting for fuel to restart that old flame.
The burned area from the season past. The fire trucks
can't get there. There's no road in. The hose won't reach
that deep inside where the bitterness is aglow. Let a new
season come. His reign over us. His word from heaven.
A mighty bolt of lightening strikes where we are most proud.
Our mighty stance, our stand. Crash, crack, crumble we come
face to face with our own dirt. The lies, the sin, the deceit, the
pain. We lay broken, pathetic in the dirt. Something dies.
Our fire of bitterness has been overcome by something
greater. Another one. Stop, recognize, consider,
attend. Which fire do we want. His or ours?
When we say no to our own voice and
Yes to His, then we have become
overcome. We try to put
out our own fires.
God never
Intended
us not
to be
ablaze.
When He is the fire within,
we don't
have to Control
the flame. The passion can burn
out of control. Passion pushes the seasons.

Soul Cry

Deep within my soul I cried for a Savior
because I needed one.
Deep within my soul, for mercy I cried.
From way on the other side, it came to me in a place
I couldn't go, wasn't authorized, no admittance,
and opened the door for me; then propped it
open with a door stop.
He put down His foot.

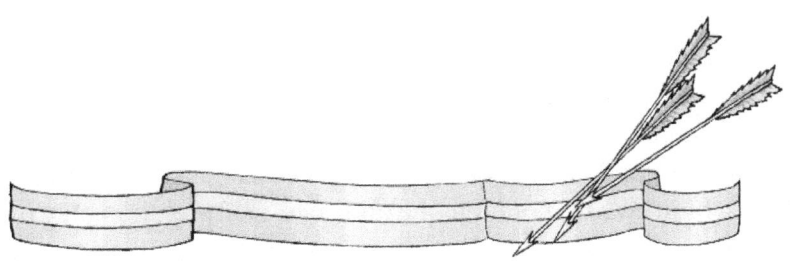

Chapter II
Indwelling

Laying Gold on our Paths

Prayer through Jesus' name is the foundation for our relationship with God. God wants to direct our lives through interactive prayer with him. He wants to build our house by coming to live within us.

But, many times, we don't come to him for direction. Instead, we try to come up with our own answers to the questions that we have.

When we trust our own thinking to come up with what we think God wants us to do, then we have built on the foundation with straw. What after that house is built, then we will attempt to live in it. It's like buying a new house. None of the old furniture fits, the stove and the dryer needs to be electric and we have brought gas. Then, there are times that we find there might be a train track three blocks away from our new house that has a train that passes at three in the morning.

We are stubborn, so we press through with our own plans for what God wants to do with our lives. We make ourselves and others around us miserable.

We make the appliances work even though they need special connections; we make the orange striped furniture go with the blue rug. We buy earplugs for the family to endure the train noise.

If we learn how to listen to the voice of God, he will unfold our path with his light. The light isn't on the outside of us, however, it comes from within when we open ourselves up to him. When we turn our lives over to the Lord, the Holy Spirit comes and lives within us. This is a mystery that only God knows the answer to. But the Holy Spirit interprets the voice of God to us in a way that we can understand it. He is the key that unlocks the door and shows us the direction to take. God continually speaks to us, only we cannot understand what he is saying except when we ask him. We do not have the ability to interpret the voice of God within our own selves.

We live in a world that is dominated by the power of Satan unless we call upon the power of God to rule. Within this world, Satan has laid a path for us that leads to further separation from God and to our own ultimate destruction. He wants us to be in bondage to his ways; to help build his kingdom of pain and suffering. When we don't pray and ask God for direction, then Satan will put thoughts in our minds as well. The pathway that God has laid out for us becomes covered over by other plans. It is like a golden road covered by slippery moss. The pathway of God doesn't disappear, but is covered over. If we pray then God removes the moss, so we can see the pathway of Gold that he has laid out for us as it was originally intended for us.

Psalms 119.127-138, Isaiah 26, John 14.23-27, 2 Peter 1.16, Revelation 3.18.

Light Knowledge

Arise and shine.
My light has come.
The light of the knowledge of who I Am.

Computation

Add it up. One life committed to Him
Becomes multiplied 3 into 1 body, soul,
spirit into Him.
There will always be a trailing number of 3.
God will continue to be magnified forever.

Sold out to Jesus

Joy and delight
E're my Savior tonight
To know him and be found in Him,
at His house, His place, not mine.
I hereby submit to you, My Lord
the deed to my house.
I have been sold
out to you.
When we have given our soul to Jesus,
why do we still rent out rooms to others?
As we turn our lives over to Jesus in a profession
of our faithfulness to Him, what does this mean?
We have relinquished ownership of
the property. Let Him do the
maintenance
on your house,
your
interior,
your lot.
Buy Eternal
Why rent when you can own.
Don't rent, buy.
Receive eternal values for ever more.
A House, a Kingdom, a New Heaven.

Bubble Gum

It comes wrapped A package with a riddle in it.
Then you chew on it The most amazing thing
happens. Bubbles. There's new air mixed
with sweetness and fun. Dreams come to
us wrapped in a package with a riddle.
When we chew on them, God
gives
us new insight into our life
mixed with the freshness
of the Holy Spirit,
amidst His sweet
surprise, He
blows up the
vision
He
has
placed
in our heart.
Bubble over
with delight, open
the
riddle, expand the message,
seek understanding of His dreams.

Move to a New Lot

The dream: I move to a new parking lot. The old parking lot is open next to a lot of trees. I have to walk a long ways to get to my house. The new parking is a marked spot in the parking garage. It is close.

Interpretation:
There is a place where we park. A spot where we usually come to rest when we go to work and home. It is our lot. The old lot is next to a bunch of trees. I imagine these are referring to other Christians. I have thought that my lot was next to them, doing what they want me to do.

But, in the dream, God says that when I park myself next to others, then I will have a long ways to walk to get to where I should call home. It is a long ways to a real place of rest for my soul. My heart will continually seek the rest that God has promised to me, and as long as I search for it in my old lot, then I will have further to walk.

He wants to move me to His lot. His lot is covered, like a covered garage within a multiple level building. He wants to bring me inside of His provisions. He wants to be the one to tell me what to do next. He has it all covered.

I Samuel 15.22, Psalm 40, Isaiah 33.13, 43, 46, 51, 60, Hosea 6.1-6, Mark 12.

Over and Above

Over and above He gave to us.
Over and above we spent it and ask for more.
Why not? There is. He has, and He gives.
It's His idea.
God's Right
God has the right to close the door to
His house any time. He can stop the draft.

The Child Within

Tremendous insight can be gained by ceasing to pretend like adults, and acting like the children we are deep within. For, when we come to God as a child, then it is much easier to accept His responses as a Father. Our need Fosters our dependence. It doesn't change our relationship with Him, only our perspective to it.

Savior Speaks in Dreams

All night long my Savior speaks in dreams. Like movie
cameras into your mind meant to not merely show pictures,
but move us from one place to another, to lead us,
direct us,
help us,
rebuke us,
encourage us, cuddle us. It's like a
voice you hear when one door is open and you are
on the other side of it. Jesus is the one who has
opened the door. He keeps it propped
open.
The Father speaks through
the Holy Spirit
in a gentle
voice to our
spirit. Listen.
Listen
to
the
Spirit.
Quiet
the flesh.
Give Him
your will. Then
your spirit is available to soar
with His to heights unknown by humans.

Neglectant Drama

How can you sleep when I'm talking to you?
But, I let you snooze while I continue to talk.
Then, you ignore me as if I never spoke.
Neglectant drama.
There's no charge for the movie.
But, at least you could stay awake during the show.

Pajama Party

It's a Pajama party with your Creator.
Dreams.
Does He have pajamas?
He picks the topics and leads the discussion.
He shows the movie projector.
He passes out the popcorn and we watch the movies in bed suspended by Him.
He dangles the lines in front of us.
We know the characters.
It's us. We are the star.

Child Like Push Pins

Light, bright,
pictures at night,
to us.
Dreams come.
Simple and childlike,
just like the push pins on a picture,
God draws the design for us.
Then, He uses it to
Push us, prod us,
and protect us.
Father, be
My light,
bright,
all
through
the night.
Reign in my life,
show me the way, I pray...

Foundation of God's House

The dream:
The Pastor of a Church and his wife are building a house. They have selected a lot. The foundations have just been laid.

I have been given the job of selecting a design for the walls of the Pastor's daughter's washroom. The color of royal blue is already present, so I need to match it up with some blue etchings that will be drawn on the walls. I leave to find an age appropriate design (one that she will like) for the walls. I go searching. As I am on my way, I end up on a side path.

There is a whitewashed fence with a garden that is overgrown with weeds. An old telephone is in the center of the garden and it rings. It is a friend I barely know. He thinks that I am not working fast enough and will not do a good job on the walls. He wants to give the job to a different person with the same name. I tell him that she is busy building her own house, then hang up on him.

Then, I go back to my car and resume my search for the design for the walls. I go through several green lights up and down rolling roadways. All of the lights are green.

Interpretation:
God wants us to start on the foundation to build the Church. He has plans for the blueprints that He wants in the 'washroom'. The cleansing of his Church needs to be matched up to the proper season.

The daughter in the dream is the Church. We need to stick to the path that He wants to provide for us now and not get sidetracked with old plans. His old plans were for that era, not for today. He is in a different stage of the building process. There will be those who will try to dissuade us from building on this foundation, but we need to stick to the process that He has set up for us. We need to be diligent to search for the design that He wants to fulfill in our life today. He desires to cleanse His people: to meet them in the wash room.

He has plans for this time: seasonal plans. We need to be careful to build on His foundation rather than our own. He will tell us what to do. When we follow His ideas, all of the lights will be green. There will be no stopping the Church that is built on the proper foundation.

We are each formed in the womb for a purpose intended by our creator. We are to be little temples to reflect the glory of God. He wants to make His presentation to the world through us. We are the framework to the picture that He wants others to see of Himself.

As there are many buildings, there are many uses for them. No wonder we don't all look the same. God is forming a Kingdom. A Kingdom has many different structures.

God is the master planner and He has the blueprints to the Kingdom. They are in his hand held by the Spirit of Wisdom. He has every detail planned right down to the place settings that are supposed to be used on his table.

First, we need to ask Him what His intended purpose for us is. What kind of a building are we? Some of us are bridges and some of us are light houses. We don't know without asking the One who holds the plans.

Next, we need to ask Him what part we play in the building of the entire Kingdom of His? Where do we fit in? Are we part of the transport team, the communications team, or the power supplies? He will tell us if we ask because He says that He will always answer when we call out to Him. Ask.

We want a building that is sturdy. It needs to be one that is formed by His plans for us. When we see other's plans and attempt to follow them using our materials then it will not work. In our neighborhood the houses are built quickly. The builder told the contractor which plan of houses to deliver as kits to which lots. Then, the contractor brought huge trucks of wood and supplies to each lot as was planned by the master builder. If the builders on site tried to build a different plan of house other than the one that the materials were laid out for, it would not work. They would have severe frustration because the supplies would not match up to the needs.

Often, we try to build our house using our own plans. But, we have no control over the building supplies. We have to use what has been delivered to our lot already. We need to talk with the builder.

Our personal foundation must be in our love for Him because of what He has done for us. He will give us instruction. I am not to build with what I think is valuable to me or books and sermons by others, but on the Words of God. Faith will enable us to look forward beyond the foundation to build the house without seeing it.

Problems with the Building

The dream warns us that there are those that will try to stop the building process. They will say that this process of learning will be too slow. It will take too much time to try to have God teach us Himself. Others, often, want us to enroll in their programs of building

But, God reminds us that He wants to lay our foundations and to grow us Himself. He has an individualized building process in mind for each of us. He does not build track homes, only custom homes.

Others may say that we are not listening to leadership when we follow our own path that God directs. They will accuse us of not following their 'Church authority' in the building process. We are not clones in the Kingdom of God. He has not called us to make disciples like 'twins' after our own image. He wants to grow us and lead us individually.

There may be those who will say that 'unlearned' Children of God can not follow His voice on their own without being under the direction of a pastor or priest. They insist that we need them to interpret God for us because we have not gone to school for it. This is contrary to the Scriptures. It is false teaching which generates dependence on men instead of God. God does want to speak to all of us individually and to train us all as His special children.

We are all anointed and all set aside for His purposes. One who has gone to a Ministry School is not 'more anointed' than anyone else. As well, their words are not 'more anointed' than any one else's' words. It is the power of God that brings the anointing: It is by Him, not us, that people's lives are changed.

Certainly, schooling to learn more about the Scriptures is beneficial because we learn more about God and His character. Concentrated study of God is wonderful. It does not, however, make us closer to God. Intimacy with God is by the Holy Spirit, not by knowledge.

There are those who will tell us that by seeking God on our own, we are diverting from the 'flock'. God says that this is not true, we are simply finding our own way to the feeding trough. Each of us must take our own trail. God comes to each of us individually. The result is the same; unity with Him through the love of God.

There may be those who are jealous of our relationship with God, when we tell them 'God spoke to me'. Our response should be to tell them, 'Talk to God yourself, you will see, He will talk back to you."

Recently, someone asked me to write a book of my 'experiences' with praying for others for healing, deliverance and raising the dead. My response was, "No." God's Kingdom is flowing. He does not want others to read about my past experiences. Not to downplay testimonial books, because they have a place, but with the mission He has given to me. He wants them to experience it for themselves. Why would you merely want to read about my relationship with God when you can have your own. It's like watching soap operas when you could have your own romance. Why would you want to settle for window shopping when you could have something real? We need to encourage others to pray for intimacy with the Father. God is equally interested in building everyone.

Ezekiel 13, Proverbs 8,9, II Corinthians 9:11

Stories By Dad

Pitter, patter
children in the hall
Where are they going?
It's a bed time story. An
enactment made alive by their
father.
It's like a play to them. They are enthralled
with his voice, the inflection of His words. Each
night there is an embrace of tenderness and intimacy
intertwined in their bedtime stories. We have taken the
candy and thrown away the box. We have kept the
story told by our Father, but do not know
the embrace of tenderness and intimacy
which comes from being intertwined
in His love.
We've forgotten how to
sit on His lap.

Foundation of Large Buildings (and Churches)

A foundation is a base that must be stable, secure, permanent and built for it's intended purpose of the builder. The Church is built like a large building. It has to be built with a foundation that conforms to the requirements of the owner for it's intended purposes.

The requirements of the owner are converted into a set of drawings with written specifications and jobs are given to those who are qualified to build that part of the structure. There are elements of a building to be considered in it's construction: The foundation provides stability, the structure supports imposed loads and transmits them to the foundation.

The exterior walls may be part of the support of the structure as well as the interior partitions. There is environmental control, vertical transport, communications, and power supplies. The building has to be able to handle 'dead' loads and 'live' loads. 'Dead' loads are the loads imposed on the building from itself.

All act directly downward, constantly and are additive from the top of the building downward. 'Live' loads are wind, seismic forces and temperature changes. If the foundation is not able to handle this, the building can settle, collapse, distort and rupture under the stress. A large building can have a small foundation if it is built on bedrock. Deep foundations are built on piles made of timber, concrete or steel that are located in clusters. They are driven down into strong soil or rock at a predetermined depth as far as 100 feet for an extremely tall building. In a multistory building, the structure is reinforced with cross timbers to provide lateral stability. The columns are connected to the girders.

Royalties

Royalties: Benefits from writing a book on the best seller's list or blessings from being the child of a King

Contemplation of Beyond

Contemplation of beyond starts now. For we have become a door to the future when we insert the key into the slot of the door of the house He has left us the deed to.

Prepare for Holy Service

To be prepared for the
service in excellence
within the presence
of the
Holy King,
You must
be
properly
dressed and taught
some
manners.
What manner
of love the Father
has bestowed on us that we
should be called sons of the Most High God

Picking Your Fruit

To awaken the sleeping bear is to rouse him from hibernation. He arises to eat berries along the sea.
Our bareness.
When we are aroused from our sleep will send us to pick God's fruits hanging by the clumps over the water.
We must arise and pick from His goodness.
Reach our hand out and bring in what He has provided for us, His children.
Oh, may we see a bigger clump of black berries down the way.
But, when we get there, we realize we have already passed over the best.
Now, we can decide; take second best, or return to what we have passed by.
God gives us a gift, a vision, a mission. Sometimes, like children, we see someone else's just beyond our reach
so we walk on.
We pass by to what we think is better.
Then, when we are there, we realize that is not for us.
We have already passed ours.
We went off the property owned by our forefathers and on to someone else's.
We are trespassers, looking to claim fruit that we have no right to.
Turn around, I did, and go back to the best.
Then pick from those berries, that fruit which hangs by the clumps over the bank by the sea.

Prune to Bloom

The more we let Him prune us, the more flowers
we will have. Sometimes we get pruning
season mixed up with the blooming.
Sometimes there's both.
Like the Rose of Sharon.
For your bloomers
to show, you
have to take
off your
skirt.
It's
OK.
Go to the dressing
room. There's one waiting
for you. It's left by the Lamb.

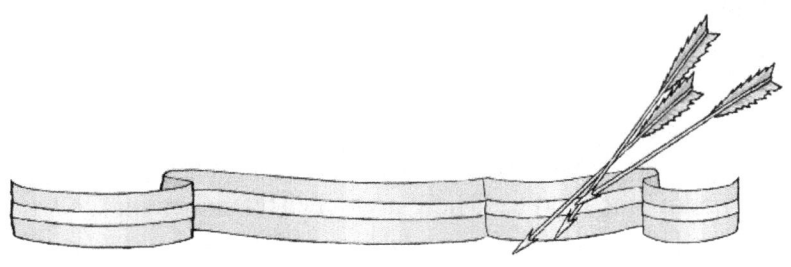

Chapter III
Rainbow of His Love

Divine revelation comes when we open our soul to the light. Remember, the light doesn't come from us because we aren't divine.

Seven Spirits of God

The Lamp Stand
A shoot will come up from the stump of Jesse; from his roots a Branch will bear fruit.
The Spirit of the Lord will rest on him, the Spirit of wisdom and of understanding, the Spirit of counsel and of power, the Spirit of Knowledge and of the fear of the Lord, and he will delight in the fear of the Lord.
(Isaiah 11.1-3)

The seven Spirits of God which are outlined in Isaiah are the presence, the Wisdom, Understanding, Counsel, Might, Power, Knowledge, and the Fear of the Lord.

God has given me dreams and insight into each of these seven Spirits. This is a preview. The *presence* is when Jesus came to earth. He is the manifest presence of the Lord. He is God come in the flesh to mankind.

There is Wisdom and Understanding. *Wisdom* is having the mind of the Lord. *Understanding* is to know why. To know what God is thinking. And, to understand why he would do things a certain way because you understand his way of thinking. (Love his heart with your heart). There is a bridge. It is 'revelation'. It provides the link between the two houses of Wisdom and Understanding. It makes us to 'get it'.

The *Spirit of Counsel* gives us direction. The *Spirit of Might* provides the power for stuff to happen. With this combination there is direction with ability to carry through by the release of his power.

There is the *Spirit of Knowledge*. This Spirit provides us with the information about who God is. There are over 100 names for God in the Scriptures. This Spirit explains who he is. The *Fear of the Lord* is the Spirit that teaches us how to respond to situations with his response because of his love for us.

The seven spirits of God are not different from God, but manifestations of him to us. They provide access to his throne from earth because they are constantly before him. He has freed us through Jesus to come before this throne.

We bring ourselves, he gives us himself; his manifestations. We have become a kingdom of priests with different dominions. He has given to each gifts; areas of authority as he desires. Each of these areas are places where God wishes to free his people from the bondage of Satan. When we are freed from our bondage of sin, we become free to follow the ways of righteousness through the Holy Spirit dwelling within us. God has removed all of our sin in a single day when Jesus Christ rose from the dead to defeat Satan's kingdom forever.

He delights to dwell within our midst. He wants a city without walls; to be the wall about us. He desires to become a wall of fire around us and to give us glory all of the time. He provides prosperity and comfort to us.

He knows that we have been eating the bread of adversity and the water of affliction because we don't know where the true bread and water are. He wants to provide his people with his true bread, the bread of his word. He wants them to be comforted and healed. God wants to bind up our bruises and heal our wounds. We need to ask him. His provision is made through his word. His breath flowing in and through us carrying his word will bring his fullness to the people.

We need to begin to walk in his Kingdom. To see the kingdom that is invisible and quit focusing on the visible kingdom. Then, he will move in a mighty way. He has given us the robe of righteousness. When we are obedient to his word, he gives us rights to govern his house, have free charge in his courts, and free access among angelic beings.

The Oil Lamp

The Holy Spirit of God has been given to us by Jesus upon his ascension to Heaven. The Holy Spirit can be compared to the oil stand in Exodus 25 that God required the Children of Israel to make as part of their temple furnishings.

The lamp stand was to be made of pure Gold. God's word to us is pure gold, refined in a fire seven times. It was to be hammered out of one piece. God's word is a hammer that breaks the rock into pieces. Every demonstration of God through Jesus Christ, God, and the Holy Spirit has been hammered out. It comes from the Word of God, one source. The lamp stand has a single base. There is but one base to all of our faith; a relationship with God through Jesus Christ based on the love of God. That is our base; that is our capstone. Jesus was hammered with the word of God by his Justice when he represented us by taking on the sin of the world, yet it only shaped him into a new representation of the glory of God. Like a solid piece of gold, he was transformed into an avenue to share God's light with the world. The Lamp stand has flowers, buds and blossoms at the same time. We have an eternal season of prosperity by the entrance of Jesus Christ into the world.

Through Jesus Christ, God has made a single stand. We are like little lamp stands as well. We stand for him and represent him with the different faces of his radiance. Each light shines a different glow from a different aspect of his character. We are all equal channels of his light to others. The provision for the light to the lamp stands is from the same source of power. The oil of the Holy Spirit flows from the Father's love into each source of light by its own channel. The oil is the fuel that burns to make the light be sent outward.

The Gold stand is upheld by his rod; his strength. The Word of God that makes us stand upright. It is the base for everything. A talent of pure gold was to be used for the lamp stand. We are to use all of our talent; the gold that he gives us to light the way in front of us within his temple.

God's love to us provides the base for the stand. When we come to know his love for ourselves, he begins to build his wisdom within us. This wisdom rises to become a light to others just like a lamp stand. There are seven demonstrations of God's light and love given to us and passed on to others. He gives to us and we become his face to the world. He gives oil and gold, we are transformed into light. (***Miracule's.***)

Ex 25:31-40, 27:20,21, Pr 6.16, 9.1, Isa 11, 30, Jer 23:29, Zech 2-4.

Wisdom is Found

Wisdom is found in a place teaming with life.
The words enter and change you.

Wisdom of Proverbs

The wisdom of God is His plan. Before we can do something, we need a plan. He does too. He has made plans for the building of His Kingdom. A long time ago, He sat down and developed plans for the earth, the heavens, and us. He already has plans on how He wants to show us His love into our lives. There are plans for how the Church is to be raised up to become his lovely bride.

As children of God, we are to become the pillars of the church. What does this mean? We are to be the ones to hold the roof up over the heads of those who need protection from the weathers of life. The only way we can become strong enough to uphold the Church is to call upon God's strength to help us. So, we want to be a pillar. Where are we supposed to stand? We need to ask Him. He is the architect, the builder, the contractor. He has the contract to build the Church the way He has planned.

Wisdom is the unraveling of the plans of God. The difference in the plans of God and our plans is that he has all the ability to fulfill them to completion. He has the supplies. He backs his word. When he says something, it is as good as done. It is through his word that the world was created. As we learn his plans, we can pray into them. It becomes as if God speaks his plans into being when we pray. His wisdom will flow through us. It brings us to total victory every time.

The house of God built through his wisdom is as good as completed because of who backs it. He wants to tell us his plans. Through wisdom the house is built, and through understanding it is established. When we hear God's voice, we need to understand it before we can obey it. Through knowledge all the rooms of God are filled with rare and beautiful treasures.

The Spirit of Counsel

One of the Seven Spirits of God.

God is as interested in our plans, as well as in the outcome of them. When we exclude Him from them, He knows. His ears and eyes are always upon His Servants, no matter whether we are doing what He wants us to or following our own paths. Our plans provide the seed for what we intend to do, so you can bet He is interested.

Maybe we listen to friends advice, the television, or our own experience to tell us what to do. When we devise a plan of action that is not taken from consulting God, then we have a 'seed' for sin. When we follow that plan, there will be problems (further sins).

If He can convince us to stop 'sin' at the seed rather than after it has grown a plant, then He will save us from a lot of hurt. The seed of sin is a plan that is not from God, but from somewhere else. For example, maybe someone has done us wrong. We plan our retaliation to that person who has hurt us. When we retaliate, he responds. We have prompted him to sin. Sin has conceived and brought forth another sin. Our seed, our plan, has yielded fruit after it's kind.

Let's be more 'spiritual' about it. Suppose we decide to become a missionary to the American Indians. We sell all our stuff and move our family to the reservation. We can't speak the language and do not have a gift of evangelism. So, we become frustrated. Our anger is transferred to our family and we start to have disputes. There is no money because God does not promise to provide for plans that are outside of His. Discouraged and despaired, we return to our old way of life. The sin of planning without God's ideas has conceived and brought forth more sins and grown a tree that we planted with our own seeds. When we plant tree, we have no ability to tend it because we do not have the power of provision in our hands.

The Holy Spirit has been given to us to provide us with counsel. When our spirit bears witness with the Spirit of God, we receive His counsel into our heart. The Holy Spirit drops things into our heart, not our mind. Our mind has to be open to receive the things of God from our heart for these ideas to become real to us.

We have no reason to feel like we are stumbling around in the dark with regard to direction in our lives from God. When we call to Him, He will offer advice from so many directions, that our way will be lit up ahead of us like a trail of fluorescent fish along the shore line. God doesn't mind giving confirmation when we are unsure which way to go. He likes to direct us. He guides us with His eye upon us. It is like we are His 'only' son. When He directs us, it is as if he Had no other children; He pays all of his attention to us. After all, we traded places with His 'only' Son. We become His 'only' children.

When God directs us, he gives us the opportunity to talk with Him about the plans. He is not like a military officer who commands his soldiers. The Lord desires to sit down with us and talk over the plans before He helps us to enact them. We need to take time to sit with Him and listen to his counsel. We wants to listen to us as well. He desires our lives to become a 'conversation' with him. He leads us like a Father leads his children.

To get direction from God into our lives, there is an interaction between the Scriptures and hearing the Voice of God into our lives for today. The Scriptures teach about who God is and his ways; his character. When we study the scriptures, we will come to know what God likes and doesn't like, so when we are presented with a decision, we will know how He would choose. His voice to us tell us what to do today. We can do with one or the other, but both is best. There are many Children of God who just listen to God through the Scriptures as they read them on a daily basis. On the other hand, there are those who have received Jesus as their Savior, yet do not read the Bible on a daily basis. These ones 'ask' Him for direction. He gives them prompting within their spirit through a gentle voice. They follow the 'voice' for direction, rather than the Scriptures. Both are right.

It is like a bowling alley. We want to keep our ball out of the gutter. When small children bowl, they have these blow up things that they put in the gutter to keep the ball from going into it. God has provided us with blow ups to keep us out of the gutter. One side is the Scriptures and the other side is the Spirit of Counsel.

When we are familiar with the Scriptures, it is like knowing someone. When you go to a restaurant, you would know to order coffee or tea. On the other hand, those who follow the voice of God, know when the friend will show up today. Those are things that are not written in the Bible, but equally important.

When God tells us of his plans through his voice to our spirit, through dreams or visions, we must confirm them through the Scriptures. The Holy Scriptures tell us of the knowledge of God. His character is constant, therefore, we will further understand his purposes when we understand his character revealed in them.

The Spirit of Council gives us advice. It is not absolutes. In the Kingdom of God there is good, better, and best. My life verses are Isaiah 1:18, 19. Most people know Isa 1:18 which says that 'though my sins be as scarlet, they shall be white as snow. Though they be red as crimson, they will be white as wool.' But, I have yet to find someone who knows the next verse. It says, "If we are willing and obedient, we will eat the best of the land."

I have asked God for a spirit of willingness and obedience to attain to the 'best' that He has for me. It is His Holy Spirit that places that spirit of willingness within us. He provides grace and provision along with it, so it is a slam-dunk deal. Win/win situation.

We can stand for 'good' or we can seek the 'best'. When we combine the Word of God with the words of God and walk into obedience of those words, we will have 'best'. We will be used by Him every minute of the day for His purposes.

Sometimes we don't understand why God is sending us a certain direction. He is asking for us to listen to his direction and become obedient to it so He can use us as part of his bigger plan. Perhaps, He is sending us the 'long way' because He has set up an individual that He intends us to talk with about salvation. When ever my schedule is changed, I become alert because I know God wants me to touch a life that I would not usually touch. The Kingdom of God is in motion.

Two days ago He had my life touch a family from Germany. The husband had a heart attack while they were on 'holiday' in Las Vegas. He was my patient. I befriended his wife and son. His sickness was extended, which meant that the son and wife continued in Las Vegas. I invited them to lunch. Then, I interpreted a dream for her. In the dream she jumps off a boat and goes down. At the bottom of the sea, she looks up and sees a light. I went and got my Bible. She was so curious about it that as I opened my Bible, she got up from her seat and came to read over my shoulder. I opened to John chapter one to show her who the light is. She was surprised to see words in red. She had never seen the 'red' words before. So, I explained to her about Jesus and His red words.

It was through her son who acted as an interpreter for the conversation. After about an hour we all prayed for salvation and the baptism of the Holy Spirit. I gave her my little book with the words in red so she could learn to love them as I do.

It doesn't get any better than that! Instead of sending me to Germany to be a missionary, He brought Germany to my kitchen table. It was only because I was listening to the Spirit of Counsel that I moved forward in the relationship with them.

Sometimes we will feel that we are going 'around the bush'. We may be tempted to go the same way we already know: To take the 'direct' way instead. If we do, then we may loose the opportunity to minister God's Kingdom to someone. His purposes will be hindered when we are not obedient; God will, no doubt, send someone else to minister to that individual, but we will loose the blessing of sharing Him with that person. We will have taken 'good' over 'best

When we wrestle with issues instead of seeking the direction from God, then our own mind becomes our enemy. There is no winner. The enemy wins without a battle.

To have complete victory over our enemies, we need to get behind the shield that God has provided. When we get on God's side, we will hate evil as much as he does. We will have no tolerance for it in our thoughts. The only thing that keeps us from going to the winning team is our own pride. Often, we think that we know a better way. We think that we don't need to come to God for help. Perhaps, we don't think that our problem is worth bugging him about. This is only arrogance on our part because God has already instructed us to come to him about everything. Pride and arrogance leads us straight into the gully away from the intended path for us.

Who ever God binds cannot be released. What ever he tears down, cannot be rebuilt. His Wisdom, Power, Counsel and Understanding bind his purposes into fulfillment. When his Kingdom is put against the Kingdom of Darkness, it is destroyed and cannot be rebuilt.

God has plans, blueprints, already written. He is waiting to pass them out to any of his Children that are willing to listen. His plans include destruction of the Kingdom of Darkness (Satan's Domain) and the absolute rein of the Kingdom of God.

There is no wisdom, no insight, no plan against the Lord that can succeed. He alone holds the key to victory. The power of God backs up his plans. When God plans something, it is as if it is already done. God does not have to wait for supplies or money to get a project done. He only waits for the people to pray in his will and be willing to be part of his plans. Mary, mother of our Savior prayed into His will. An angel came to her and told her that she would have a son. Her reply was, "Be it according to His will." She was told of a plan of God, and she prayed it into action, then walked into it.

When we discover some of the 'blueprints' of God's plans, then it is as if the building is already built. That is faith in the word of God and the power of God to complete his word. If we do not stand firm in our faith, we will not stand at all because it is a spiritual Kingdom that we cannot see. The whole thing is a faith venture.

When God wants to fulfill one of his purposes, he will speak to one of his children who is listening to him and tell him what to do. He is like a father standing in a park calling to his children to gather to himself. When He calls to his own, they do not know why He calls until they get there. When they come closer, then He gives more instruction. As they draw near, He talks to them and sends them on what ever errand that he desires. He only desires us to listen to his voice and become obedient to it. This provides the furtherance of his Kingdom. We are the hands of God reaching out to the World. It is as if God were making his entreaty through us to others.

God makes promises to us, then swears by them using His Name; the Name of Jesus. His plans have two unchangeable hopes. We hope in what we know to be true from the history of God disclosed in the Scriptures, the Bible. And we hope in the active Word of the Holy Spirit into our spirit as a child of God. They are both based on His Word and the Name of Jesus. Jesus has been given all power and authority to carry out the plan of God by His death, burial and resurrection from the dead. Both are unmovable anchors that not only confirm the plans of the Kingdom of God, but have the power to enact them.

God doesn't just tell us what to do, then go back to heaven. He guides us. Like a father holds onto the hand of his daughter. As long as we hang onto him, he will hang onto us. When we let go and start to walk off on our own, his hand is still extended waiting for us to run back to him. Often, we don't run back until we get overwhelmed. We are like a small child when something catches our eye. We run apart from our parent to check it out. Then, often, like that child, we get lost and can only see the knees of others. We become lost in the crowd unable to find our way back to the secure hand of the Father. We need only to call out to Him and He comes to us. No matter how long we have been gone, lost in the crowd looking at knees, when we call He will be there for us. He is waiting.

    Psalms 13, 33,73,107,119, Proverbs 1,8,11,15,19,21, Isaiah 7,8,11,19, 22, 29, 46, Job 12.13, 38.2, 42.3, Romans 11.34, I Corinthians 4.5, Hebrews 6.17.

Shop His Movie Mall

Girl, where have you been?
The Mall, the movies, the make-up counter.
Come to My mall, My hall and watch My movies.
I'll take up, up, up and away.
Why shop here when you can shop in Heaven?
Desires fulfilled, credit prepaid by Him.
The generous Father doesn't just drop us off at the door.
He shops with us helping to select and fulfill all our needs.
Let's go to the Mall, one store house after another,
open 24 hours a day.
Free to the kids of the owner,
your papa, your Lord, Your God, Your Abba.

Free Credit

I change for nothing.
Freely I came. Freely I give.
Because I am in charge, I own all the credit.
Be magnified O My soul for your Redeemer
lives to make His righteousness complete in you.

Lamb's Wool Sweater

Ba, Ba, Black sheep, Does he have any wool?
No. It's only given by the white one.
That one's been sheered. The white one controls the sheers.
He's held to be the provider of our wool. Let's make a sweater.

Old Fashioned Time Wrapper

Oh, to have those who live the love,
To do what I have only dreamed of until
they are willing to go out on that limb for Me.
The place I dwell is surrounded by miracles because
of My power. It is Me. I
created your world,
but I live in Mine. I come to yours
by invitation. I am a sensitive type and usually
don't go where I am not invited. It's not that I
don't want to be with My children, But they
have shunned Me. They are like teens
running off to their 'good time.'
Without inviting their father.
They think I am not
like them.
I'm
old fashioned and
don't understand them.
They forgot that I was
once their age. And, I remember
it as yesterday, because I wrap time.

Eating Like a Lamb

Sometimes, I feel like a lamb.
And that God gives me food on a plate
at the table of His presence.
Then, I chew, and chew.
I nibble the grass on my plate at the table.
I don't need any dressing,
because He brings the oil for the salad.
The grass is served at His table on a glass plate
that the Son shines through to us.
His revelations shine through because
 of the Holy Spirit that was sent to us through
the provision of Jesus Christ.
Our heart is the glass plate that He is able to write on.
As we come to His table,
He gives us revelation after revelation,
like an all you can eat salad bar to a lamb.

Conception Conversation

At which point do we go from, not existing,
to becoming eternal?
When your soul became a living soul.
But when was that?
When I made you.
When we were first conceived?
Was it before we were finished?
Child of Mine, you won't be finished
until you enter My presence in heaven.

Prudence at the Table

Where's prudence?
Seated next to contentment next to delight.
There are many.
They are all on the same
side of the table like the 12 disciples in that picture.
Remember, Jesus is in the middle?
The table of My presence, where I Am.

The Spirit of Might

Words: *God brings His healing seven ways.*
Leading by God takes us His way, in his time.
The day of atonement came three times. She came in the clouds.

Healing Seven Ways

God heals by his seven spirits. When God shows up, all of him comes. He does not just bring part of his presence. It's like when we show up for dinner at someone's house, we bring all of ourselves. We bring our body, our mind, our emotions, our problems; all of us.

As we pray and seek our place behind the robe of Jesus, then the presence of God will come to us. The robe of Jesus provides the grade we need to come to the Lord's table and eat of whatever he eats. We are no longer slaves, but he calls us his Children and the brother and sister of Jesus. He made this provision 2000 years ago. He planned it since eternity past to show us his love.

The same provision is for us today. He provides his Holy Spirit to give us his presence daily, now. And, he will come again to bring us to himself. He has provided three atonements. One past, one present and one in the future. All come in the clouds. The rescue of God comes in the clouds. We need to look up; seek Heaven for the answers.

The healing of God comes through the cross. The Cross of Jesus Christ that was given for us. He comes to us to meet our needs. When he crosses over us at the point of our need, then we are healed. He meets us at the heart. There is a cross over. His cross is over our heart. We bring our cross; our burdens to him at his Cross. He provides healing and forgiveness. His cross bears our cross at the point of our need; our heart. The healing starts in our heart.

It is like an EKG of the heart. When an EKG is taken it is pictures from 12 vantage points that all point to the center of the heart. It is like the heart is suspended when these pictures are taken. A cross is equidistant from the base to the arms. (Lay on the floor and measure to prove it to yourself.) If we take two crosses and place one horizontal and the other vertical, then make them meet, there will be six nails that are separated at equal distances from the heart. Now run a spear through the heart like a skewer. That is what Jesus did for us.

We must lift his Cross up. Elevate his Cross in our mind and lives. Then lay down our own cross. We are to lay down our own desires and lift up his. We lay down our burdens. So, we become the horizontal cross. Then, open our heart to him. Let him pierce our heart with his love. He has made this provision for us. He received the spear so that we would not have to.

Flow to others

The Spirit of Might is a flow Spirit. It is the flow of the power of God to others. God's Spirit comes to us two ways. When we ask him to indwell us, the Holy Spirit come to live inside of us. He makes his home within us. We become the temple of God by his Spirit that he has made to dwell within us.

When a Brother is moved by the Holy Spirit to speak words from God, then the Holy Spirit flows through him to us. When this happens, the Holy Spirit comes to us from this brother. The Holy Spirit that dwells within us bears witness to the testimony that the words are from God. The two Spirits collide. They kiss; they clap. They laud God. Often, we get 'goose bumps'.

The Spirit of might flows through us when we proclaim the words of God to others. It is about the flow.

One of God's names is 'Healer'. He calls himself our deliverer and healer. He brings his healing seven ways. Seven is His perfect number. When people are healed, they are not healed by our hand. No one has ever healed another except God alone. No doctor ever healed. They can train and perform procedures that help the body to heal. But, God alone brings healing.

In order for the Spirit of might to flow we need to go to those in need; go to their house instead of trying to bring them to ours. We bring the presence of God to them. Then, we bring the essence of Him. When we dwell 'in Christ' then when we arrive, we bring his perfect gift. Him. We bring the complete present because all that he is, he has given to us. He makes himself known to others through us.

What we bring is perfect as we are perfect because of Christ living within me. It is just like perfect shoes delivered right to the door of your house. When God brings his healing, it will fit the individual perfectly. It is like the glass slipper that fit only Cinderella in the bedtime story. Every one of his Children he treats like Cinderella when it comes to his healing.

God will bring perfect direction, teaching, counsel, power, and might.

When we look at the person, we see their needs in the flesh. Often, we look at the eternal (shell) and ask for healing. We look with our physical eyes. God wants us to ask him to open our spiritual eyes to see what needs to be healed. There is spiritual, physical and soul healing. Often, we disregard the other two areas.

When he opens our spiritual eyes, then he will provide a destination for us to pray toward. When he leads us in prayer, then we can follow that trail to lead to healing.

As a helper of another person, we need to remember to 'move out of the way so that the individual can get on the elevator.' Often we are standing in front of the elevator door and others cannot get on the elevator. The elevator is the vehicle that takes them up to the floor that they need to be on. It is what God wants to work with them to move them into his presence. If we are standing in-between their relationship with God, then it will impede their healing. God wants to speak to each of us individually. So, as you show the person the trail to their healing, then follow the trail back to the parking lot yourself. Back out of the room, and back out of their time with God. Let them talk to him themselves, so it will become their healing. One of the worst mistakes we can make is to allow someone to think that he needs to come to us for his message from God, or his healing. He needs to seek it for himself; then it will become their testimony, not ours.

The Rescue of God Breaks Through.

The rescue of God breaks through like he broke through the water and parted it for the Children of Israel to be led out of Egypt.

When the eyes of our heart are opened and we see his brokenness as it truly is, then it will break through to our heart. None of the bones were broken on the body of Jesus, but he was broken. He was broken beyond human repair. His Spirit was crushed, and he was emotionally wounded. When we open ourselves to see him as he is, then as his brokenness comes to us it will reach that place that exists only in the mind of God. This is faith.

When I hike in the mountains near Las Vegas, along the trail there you can look off in the distance and there are two mountain peaks. At a certain place on the trail, it looks as if they are one mountain and a person could stand in the 'saddle' between the peaks. They are both sickle shaped and form a perfect U from this vantage point. I have prayed that God will help me to stand in that 'saddle' between those peaks. The only thing between those two peaks is air.

The Holy Spirit is air. So we need to learn to stand on him. But often, when we do what he wants us to do, we feel like we are out on a limb; on thin air. This is where God wants us to be; reliant on the Holy Spirit completely. So, several times, when I have prayed for something, I have prayed that God would put me between those mountains, in the place of faith, and that I would stand on air in the high place that he has planned for me. The places that God wants us to go are out of our reach and beyond our thinking. They are high places where our feet will never touch the ground. He wants us to depend on him totally.

The wounds of Jesus

He was pierced for our transgressions, he was crushed for our iniquities; the punishment that brought us peace was upon him, and by his wounds we are healed. Isaiah 53.5

Since we are surrounded by so great a cloud of witnesses, let us lay aside every weight and sin that clings so closely and run with perseverance the race that is set before us; looking to Jesus the author and perfector of our faith...Hebrews 12.1-3.

The Spirit of Might has to do with the 40 stripes that Jesus endured before he was hung on the cross. As Isaiah says, 'it is by the wounds, we are healed.' The whipping encircled his whole body. He was beat with a whip and with a cane. He was beaten. Like a cake mix. Certain bare ingredients went into the mixture, then something different came out the other side because he was willing to be beaten. He was separated. He was separated from himself. His flesh was separated from his body. It was torn off. His flesh was separated, so that our flesh doesn't have to be. He was wounded, so that we could be healed. There were wounds through and through, top to bottom, in and out from one end to the other. He left no part of himself not wounded, so that we could have total healing available to us.

He took his cup and poured it into ours. He was an open valve.

Yet, we still have wounds that are not healed. Many tell us to let Jesus take these burdens from us. But, he does not release the weights, we must let go. We are hanging onto them waiting for our healing from another direction.

We have wounds that are not healed. They are sort of healed, but not totally. They have healed with bad scar tissue. They are crusted over; filled with granulation tissue. It is like we are seeing through these wounds. We see life through the experiences that we have had in the past. They are like wounds that have been inflicted on us. We go to counseling and read books seeking healing. We go to healing services, and pray. Yet, we are not totally healed. The wounds have healed, but not totally. It is because we are looking through the scar tissue; we see through scales (like scales of bad skin). The eyes of our heart are looking through our own scales. We have measured our own healing according to our own scales instead of seeing the scales of God and measuring against the healing that he wants for us. We are using our own scales. He wants the scales to fall from our eyes.

We have allowed Satan to sneak in and steal our joy. We have a relationship with God, but the joy has been sucked out of it because we continue to be sick and in need of a physician. God wants to free our heart to sing. He wants to free the singers. He wants to unleash the tune that our heart desires to sing. He wants to take the weights that are on it. He wants to lift the scar tissue from those areas where it has been built up.

The race is easier to run without weights. What ever we have tried to heal on our own we need to send it to Jesus. He paid the price. He's the author and the perfection of our faith walk. It's about getting our heart to sing. Our heart can't sing with Jesus' heart if it wearing handcuffs. It needs to be released first. The hearts need to be released to praise.

Our praise is being held by things unknown to our present mind.

By his stripes we are healed. He was beat so that we won't be. If we lighten up we can go higher. This is for those who want not only to be alive, but live; not merely breath, but run in the race. We're looking for the crown. Jesus has made provision for all of us to be winners. He took all of that beating so that we would be winners all the time.

It is our own dirt that slides on us. He has given us all the authority to take authority over the dirt in our lives. As he sent the apostles out two by two, he gave them authority and provision. He continues to give us authority and provision. We are to find a friend, and escape from the devastation. He as made a provision, just like he made a provision for the animals in the flood as he sent them two by two. We need to find a friend and help one another to get to the place where we can be freed and released to praise God with our heart.

The Riches of God Released.

If the riches of God were released when Jesus rose from the dead, Why don't I have them?
Jesus said that we have not because you ask not. When you ask, you ask for the wrong reasons. (James) We have the wrong purposes when we ask, so he does not answer us.
We need to get our purposes in line with him, then we will have all of the riches from heaven released.
The right reason is for us to turn from the old way to his new way. We want to be the friend of God instead of the friend of the world.
When we follow his mold in prayer for healing, it is like a key that fits into a big steel door on a penitentiary. We need to align ourselves with his mold. It is like a lock and key.
When we get it right, the door will open with a rumble and a crash. God doesn't want to make us over, but fit to us. Every nook and cranny.

Love Volley

E're such delight
in my Savior tonight
to know him,
love Him,
be found in Him, and Him in me.
Awesome interaction, with above,
from below, initiated by Heaven
for us so we could sent it back
His way.
What a wonderful volley.
Love, Love. Tie it up.

Why We Tremble

Tremble in His presence. The Savior bring His reign
when He comes to the forest. His Holy Spirit drops the
rain on the leaves that help them
to move. It is His presence, His authority,
and
our position
In intimacy that stirs our heart into
Removing the dust from our
leaves,
And moving us toward
His tree of life.
And, we tremble,
We stir, we
feel
weak
inside.
But,
that's
OK,
as long as
He stays in charge.
For, he does not need
us to be strong. He is our strength.

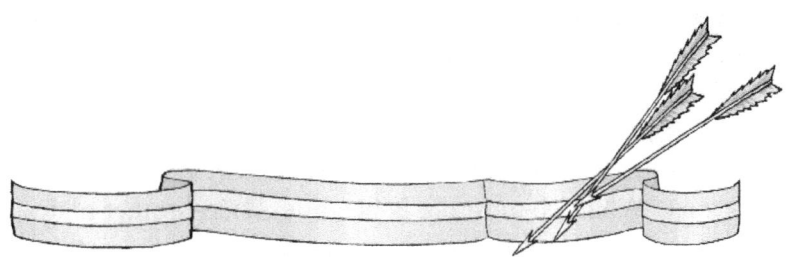

Chapter 4
The Match

The match was met when Jesus showed up.
The match made in Heaven.
Fire sent down!
O Glory!

Holiness

Holiness is a process. We have a measure of holiness here on earth, and walk toward ultimate purity to be able to enter heaven and be with God at His place. At the end of the road to holiness God has His house. It is where the throne, the rainbows of color, and the singing for ever more are. There is no evil, no sin, no darkness, no judgment, nothing vile in the presence of God. There is only laughing, beautiful singing, colors, and joy.

From His throne originates light, love and truth. The only way we can know holiness is to ask Him what it is, for there is nothing holy here on earth. The earth was tainted with sin when Adam and Eve were tricked by the Serpent in the garden of Eden.

There is a road to holiness that was paved by Jesus. He was God, so he was holy. When he died, he made a provision for us to experience the holiness of God. We can enter into his kingdom because Jesus left his coat for us. He became our brother when he came down from heaven and was born on the earth. He took on human form and became flesh. So, he bridged the gap between flesh and spirit, and between sin and holiness.

He has left us a coat with a lining called grace. It is like a thick winter coat that protects from the icy winter weather in Alaska. If we put on the coat that he left for us, then when God looks at us, he does not see who is under it, only the coat. We have the lining of his grace against our skin, so we will not be frozen from the frigid stare of the Lord as he looks on our sins. What we must do, is become a step-brother of Jesus and ask him to borrow the coat so that we may enter into the holiness of the Lord. He does not mind, he left it here on the hanger for us on purpose, so we can use it any time we need to. It is like a winter cabin in the forest. He has left it stocked for us, if we should arrive when he is not home.

The problem is that the door to the cabin is locked.

He has left the key hidden waiting for us to come along in our season. We cannot find it without some light. There is no light here on earth apart from what God provides.

Jesus claimed to be the light, and indeed he was. He has left us a piece of himself. A torch to hold in our hand to light our way. We need to light that torch to be able to see the way to the key. Ask for God to illumine the path to his holiness.

Look with God

Be magnified, O my soul.
Expand your image of who God is and who you are by Him. Look at Him, look at you. Then uncover the other I, and look together.

Bequeathed

Marriage matters most because we were bequeathed before time.

Mirrors of Praise

He wants a   duet.   His words,
our voice, our words. So you can't tell
who is who.   Intertwined.   Reflect Him.
He's the   water. He reflects   with the sea.
Look.
When we mirror Him, we bring praise
to Him
when we see what He
wants us to
be.

Joy Flows

Joy in Jesus flows from the spirit.
His Spirit to our spirit.

My Lights

Light bright, mine tonight,
Be found, I in Me, and Me in thee.

Dance with My Love

Pick the flower and dance, my Child
Dance in my Love.
Pick my essence, smell My fragrance.
Dance, sing, waltz, three step.
Come to the Father through Jesus,
the Son, and carry the Spirit with you.

Fill Your Wagon
...with Beautiful Flowers from God's Nursery

Dream:

I wake up passing God on the way to the Plant Nursery. I have a red wagon. He asks me if I have received any today? I say, "No."

Then he takes me into the Nursery and fills me up with flowers. Beautiful flowers.

Anointing

Often times we think anointing is given to a select group of believers who get a special gift from God. We think of it like a touch by a fairy's wand. They have told us that, "God called me." We think that we need a burning bush or a Holy visitation to be anointed.

This is not true. There is anointing waiting for all believers who seek Him, and are obedient to His words. To be anointed means that we have been set apart for a specific purpose. God has a purpose for each of us; a job in His Kingdom. Only, most of the time, we are the last ones to figure out what it is.

He tells us to love Him with all our heart, soul, and strength. When we first become believers we learn steps to love Him with our heart. Then, as we get our mind into the Scriptures, we start to become changed. Our soul starts to love Him. Funny how our feet follow our heart and soul.

It is like when we walk from one green field to another. One field may be a field of oats and the other of rye grass. We walk from area to the other. The first area is founded on oat seeds; these are the seeds of your own thinking: The way that you have been taught since you were small. You have built your ideas around these seeds of thought. An example might be, "Pull yourself up by your own bootstraps." From this idea you put yourself through school and didn't depend on anybody for anything.

But, as you walk into what God has for you, you come to a point where your thinking starts to change. The seeds change from oats to rye grass. The seeds of the Scriptures start to grow in your mind. Perhaps you learn the verse that says, 'Trust in the Lord with all your heart. Do not depend on your own insight..." You start to change your ways of thinking about dependence on God. You have left the field of oats and entered into the field of the rye grass; you have began to walk into the anointing that God has already laid out for you. Then you can love Him with all your heart, soul and strength.

We see those with 'an incredible anointing'. Actually, they are just further into the rye grass field. They have allowed their minds to be transformed with the seeds of the Scriptures and their feet to walk in obedience further into the field that God has planned for them. We all have an incredible anointing because our God in an incredible God!

Become Empty

When we enter the Kingdom of God we become purified unto holiness. Then, we become anointed. To become anointed is to be set apart for a specific purpose and given a direction within that purpose. God is like a container that fills us up. We must come to Him with openness to be ready for Him to fill us up. We have to empty ourselves of what we are holding onto in order to have empty hands to do whatever He asks us to do. If our hands are already full of doing what we think that we are supposed to be doing, then we will not be available to do what He asks.

He is the beaker that holds all that we need for the service He wants to put us into. He will overflow to us.. The Holy Spirit will provide guidance to us. When He fills us, the anointing comes as part of the package. We are to become little cups, having been poured into by Him, we then are poured out to others. Our cup is filled with what ever the Lord has given us for an job within the Kingdom of God. Whatever we hold in our hand to use for God. It is a cup, not a glass because it must have a 'handle' that is held by God.

When we learn to hear His voice and walk in obedience to it the oil of His joy will flow into our cup. Then, there reaches a point when our cup is full to overflowing and starts to overfill. If this cup, this anointing is near others, then it spills over to them. We walk in the reason that we were made. Our heart begins to actually sing. Others will notice.

Share

The anointing is meant to be shared with others, that God will be praised. It is meant to be our tithe to the Kingdom of God. A perpetual joy comes as we walk with His anointing in His presence. There is an anointing waiting for each of us. He has place a flask of oil on the table of His presence right next to the bread. When the message finally soaks in, the love of God soaks is like oil to dry skin. His love goes straight to our heart to become the foundation and strength.

We are the hands of God on the earth.   We are sent by God, and obedient to be His messenger, one out of a thousand, to tell a man what is right for him, to be gracious to him and say: spare him from going down to the pit. We tell one another about the provision of the grace of God through the love of Jesus Christ.

We have come to him as a child ourselves, so we are able to tell others how it is done. We expend ourselves for the message.

Mary Anoints and is Anointed

The oil is like a flask that must be broken and opened to be used. It comes with a cost to the one who has it. Mary anointed the feet of Jesus before she was anointed. She demonstrated from her heart emotional involvement. She wept.

She allowed her heart to be moved by his presence. When we get in the position where there is anointing of the feet of others, then there is a fragrance of God that is released. Then, she used her hair to wipe the oil off of his feet. Each strand of our covering needs to be washed in the presence of the Savior. Just as she wiped his feet with her crown, her hair. It brushed his feet as it flowed down. We need to pour out what we value most and let us anoint it. Allow him to purify all of our outflow. All I value most, I must put it at the feet of Jesus and let it be anointed for his service. Let my covering be his covering.

What comes out of my head, my hair, should be put to the test. I must bring it into his presence with tears and anointing. What falls onto my shoulders, I must lay at his feet. Take it all to him. As she anointed him with tears and inner cleansing, bringing her gift, he anointed her because of her position and place at his feet. She was humble and obedient.

She expended herself. She was open and broken before him first, then others. She didn't care for others, but set her mind to do what was right. She was anointed because what flowed out of her, she purposefully brought to the feet of Jesus. She worshipped him with her adornment. She planned her union with Jesus. She knew who he was and took her relationship with him personal.

I am sure that she had often sat at his feet. She knew that these were the feet of God. She knew his purpose for coming to the earth was to die for her sins. His feet were to anointed because they were to carry out the walk to fulfill the plan. The feet gave him the ability to walk in the right direction.

The Lord longs to draw people using his love as a banner. We are the ones to do the drawing as his hand is upon us. When we walk in the anointing that he has given us, the five fold ministry will develop the Church.

Genesis 8.11, Deuteronomy 14.23, Nehemiah 8, Esther 9.22, Job 33.26, Psalm 4.7, 28.7, 45.7, 71,104, 133, Isaiah 12.3, 56, 60, 61,65, Jeremiah 11.16, Zechariah 4.3, Luke 10.21, John 3.29, 15,16,17, Hebrews 1.9, I Peter 1.8, Romans 11, Galatians 4,5, James 3.12.

Unleash our Mold

'On the day you unleashed our mold,
Oh what a glorious day!'
Light of the risen Savior shines on us today.
Light of the knowledge of who He is.
Be ours, as we are yours.

Sacrifice and Atonement

What is the difference between sacrifice and atonement?
Sacrifice is to give on behalf of another when it is not required by the one who gives. It was a payment due by the other person. Their debt was paid. Atonement is the price that was paid.
How much did it cost?
It was the sacrifice of Jesus, His death on the cross
provided the complete atonement for our sins.
He paid the whole debt off.
 Not partial, but total. And we are debt free, now. His red ink provided us to be in the black.

Sweet Jesus

Thank You Israel, for sharing sweet Jesus,
Lover of my soul, Delight of my heart,
Sweet music to my ears.
Now and forever more, on and on,
because He cares.
Who cares?
He cares.
Why?
Who knows? We know.
Why?
Nothing known to us could never
negate anything He is.

Grafting into Israel: The true branch

The dream:
There are two rows of chairs. A Jewish friend of mine has been invited to come and pray. She arrives wearing a maroon kimono with a black sash. She comes in and kneels on a kneeler bench in the center. She starts to pray fervently.

As she prays, I lean over and elbow the woman next to me saying, "Look at the changes that God has made in her life!"

Then, the power of God hits me and I realize how amazing it is that He saved me, too. I fall to my knees and start thanking God for changing my life. Then, he touches the whole line of women on both sides and they fall to their knees and pray one by one.

(This Jewish friend came to me last year and asked me about Jesus. She has received Jesus Christ as her Savior.)

Interpretation:
The two rows of chairs are the two branches. My friend represents the Jewish people. They are the original olive branch and the Gentiles have been grafted into their relationship with God through Jesus Christ.

Both branches were separate, But they come together through repentance and the blood of Jesus.

God says, "When Israel was a child, I loved him, and out of Egypt I called my son. It was I who taught Ephriam to walk, taking them by the arms; but they did not realize that it was I who healed them. I led them with the cords of human kindness, with the ties of love; I lifted the yoke from their neck and bent down to feed them. Their sins have been their downfall."

We both now claim the same promises. Because, when we cry to God, he will heal us. It is the same heart rending that he has been asking the Children of Israel to do ever since he chose them as a People for his own possession. He wants us to also, rend our heart and turn to him with unrestrained passion.

As Israel was his first child, he now calls us his children. It is the vision of God to restore his children to him; to restore David's fallen tent. In the days to come, the reaper will be overtaken by the plowman for He has chosen to make us the tent.

The ability for all to be restored comes through clothing ourselves in the righteousness of Jesus Christ. We must be adorned with His sacrifice for their sin (crimson robe) and the belt of faith (black sash). It is by grace that we are all saved through faith in his provision.

He wants us to obey what he tells us to do. We are not to be arrogant regarding others who are blind but consider his kindness to us. We should not be conceited. It is by his mercy that we are saved. Our mercy is a result of Israel's disobedience. God's mercy continues to them and to us. Think of ourselves with sober judgment and with the measure of faith that God has given to each. For God has bound all men over to disobedience to that he may have mercy on them all.

Isaiah 11.5, Hosea 11.14, Joel 1, 2.12-3.32, Amos 8.9, Obadiah, Micah 4-6, 7.8-20, Zephaniah 1.6-18, 2.1-3, Haggai 1, 2 , Zechariah 1.1-6, 9.1-14.21, I Peter 5.5, 3.8-12, Romans 11, 12.

Washing with the Word of God

The
Word of God
washes us from sin.
How does the word wash?
It's like we stand under the faucet.
When we get into the flow of his word
it starts to wash over us It comes through us
and we start to change. Our words mix with his
out the other side. Mixing.
The more we stay under the water, the more pure we become.
It's still some of us coming off. It's like hair dye they we wash
our hair afterwards. Always a little washes off with each time
we put our head under the flow.
The water becomes more and more clear as the hair
continues to be washed. The more we stay in the water
(the word) the more
clean we become.
We are in a process of
holiness. We are holy and are
becoming holy. As we grow there is more

of Him and less of us. The deficit is filled with grace.

Relationship With Jesus

Words: *All foundational basic truths must be built on a relationship with Jesus Christ*

God loves us. He desires our company intense. When our relationship with him was ruptured through the sin of Adam, the opportunity for him to be close to us came to an end. The sin of Adam was not a 'mistake'. God knew ahead of time his plans and what would happen. The sin of Adam made it possible for him to demonstrate his love to us. The Holiness separates us from him because of our sinful nature.

He is the only one that is Holy, so he was the only one who could intercede between. Sin demands death as a penalty. Jesus paid the penalty for our sin. But Jesus was God. So, in essence, God paid the price for our sin all by himself. His desire for communion with us is what caused him to pay this price. So he is ever waiting in the wings for us to come to him. He has made every provision on his side to pave the way for us to have communion with him.

Jesus becomes the cornerstone and the capstone. He is the first and the last. He meets us at the cross; our point of need, and he is coming back again to purify us completely. The foundation of our relationship with him and others must be built on these principles. The church's foundation must also be built on them to survive the test of Satan's trials.

It is to be built on the 'rock' in order to be eternal. The love of God is eternal. God, himself laid a Stone in Zion, a tested stone, a precious cornerstone for a sure foundation; the one who trusts will never by dismayed. He has set the foundation on the holy mountain. It is the place of meeting with him in prayer. The Lord God Almighty loves those gates more than all other dwellings. The Most High himself will establish the Church because he loves her just like a bride is loved by her espoused husband.

Prayer is what gives us the ability to link with God and others. Prayer is communion with God. It is impossible to build a relationship with someone without talking to them. We may learn all about him from others; we may learn what he likes and dislikes, but we will never know him until we start having conversation with him. It is like reading the tabloids about the Movie Stars. We can learn 'all about' them without knowing them personally.

The only way to get to know God is through conversation with Him. The Holy Spirit is our interpreter to help us understand God.

When we individually become holy temples for God to dwell, then link with one another, we become a grand building called the Church.

Building the Church

The Church is built on the apostles and the prophets. Why? An apostle is one sent from God with a message. A prophet is one who has learned to hear the voice of God. The apostle has the message and the prophet has the interpretation. A message that has no interpreter is not worth much. Both are needed to understand what God wants the Church to do to complete the building process.

As a team, they form the basic foundation of the Church. God wants his whole church to be as sturdy as the foundation. He desires all of us to learn to hear his voice and become sent with a special message.

Jesus has made it possible for us to talk to God because of the Holy Spirit which he gave us as he went to Heaven. It is through a relationship of learning how to abide 'in him' and him 'in us' that the building of the Church is joined together. We are individuals, but he wants us to link together just like a human body. He is the head, the brains of the operation, and we are the rest. We need to learn how to link up so that we can know what we are supposed to do. Each of the parts of the body of Christ are similar to a human body. Our body cannot walk if it is not connected. We need our legs attached to the torso, to be able to walk. In the same way, Jesus is calling us to connect with each other, no matter how different we may feel that we are, so that the entire body of Christ will be able to walk.

God doesn't live in buildings, but within our souls. So, what we are talking about is a soul link, not a physical link. A spiritual link that can only happen when we link into the Holy Spirit and the other parts of the Body are also linked to the Holy Spirit. Then it will become a building built by God, not by us.

Bible and the Word

Just like the three kings, we are to
worship the baby. Worship Jesus, worship Him,
His Word, His desires, for, He is the Word. He is the
Word who became flesh for us, so that we could understand
who God is. Jesus is God. He is the exact representation of who
God is. Therefore, we worship Him as God, because He is. All that
He says, is Him, and He is all that He says, He is. They are the same.
So, do we worship the Bible? The Bible is words, written in a language
that we understand, Given in pictures that we comprehend, so that we
can know God. It is Him speaking through the hearts, minds and hands
of men through the Holy Spirit. Do we worship the words of God,
or God? The Bible is a book, God is a person. Our relationship
is to be with a person, not a book. When we love someone,
do we love them, or what they say? Are there times
when neither of you talk, you simply
spend time together?
Of course.
The same is
true with God.
We trip
when we
attempt to
describe all that God is by using a single book.
For, there
is so
much
more to Him.
And, to a
relationship with Him.
Teach us to be quiet, dear Lord.
And to enjoy the times when no one is speaking,
we are just enjoying hanging out. You and me. For it is in those
times, you sing into my heart with your heart love songs. And it feels good.

Soul Checker

Take my
soul, Dear Lord.
I don't need it any more.
For, when you are the keeper of my soul,
it's like checking a coat into
a coat closet before
an elegant dinner.
Pain and despair
drove me to hunger.
Then you invited me to dinner.
When I arrived, I realized I was overdressed.
So, I started removing the layers of clothes I had put on.
Layer by layer I hung them on the coat rack next to the door I came through.
I hoped no one would notice how many layers I wore. So overdressed.
Then, I got to my shawl: My shawl. "It's mine," I said to myself.
My grandmother gave this elegant shawl to me to have and to keep.
So I did. For years. But, then, I passed by the door.
It's a second door, a door of greater understanding into the
Depths Of God Himself. And He called out.
Just like a servant, He stopped me with His voice
and beckoned me to leave that shawl with Him.
At first, I held onto it.
It was all I had left between me and mine.
What I thought I owned. Others were
doing it. I looked into the closet
and saw rows of souls
that were being held
in safe keeping by Jesus.
So, I checked it with Him. He
has it now. He is holding it for me.
And, I went into the place to dine with
the Father. I dine at His table feasting
on His delicate love. He gives me
bites, one at a time.
Finger foods.
Small demonstrations of
His love and mercy. I don't miss
my soul. I know where it is. In His closet.
And I have the receipt. So, whether He returns
it or I pick it up as I leave, I know, until then, it is safe.

Check In Closet

Everlasting righteousness is yours eternally
because Jesus bared his soul
to the whole world.
He shared
Himself.
He opened up his walk in closet.
The place where his garment is kept.
He unlocked the door and gave us the key.
Anyone may go to that closet. It's a closet of prayer.
And ask Him for something to wear. It's like an eternal
coat closet when you pick up your coat after a party.
We can pick up our coat from the team
at the door.
The only difference is we never checked a coat in.
We don't bring one with us. He just provides.
Righteousness freely given to us
one by one
when we go to
the check in closet.

His Fish School

Fish swim together in schools. Why can't we?
Become a fish. Drenched in his love. Caught
Up in his net. Hooked by His presence.
Held in The hand of the great fisherman.
Hook and line. Let him Talk
You into getting
into his
boat.
Lay down
at his feet.
He
won't eat
you, just consume
you. It's a row boat. He
has the oars. Get in and lay down.

Forgiveness Slide of Jesus

The Dream:
Paul and I are in a water park. There is snow everywhere. We have fun. We go up and down the rides sliding and climbing. When we come to the end, I went out on a ledge. He calls me back to a better way. At first I am skeptical, then I go his way. There is a loud thunder noise. A lot of people leave the water park in a hurry, running. I didn't know they were even there because I didn't see them before. We go for a final ride down a slide. It looked like it was going to be tough but it wasn't. The snow was there to pad the way. We go to the center to gather our stuff and they couldn't find it. Eventually we find it under a bench. It is a towel and a stethoscope without ear pieces.

Interpretation:
God has an adventure waiting for us. He wants us to have fun in our relationship with him. When we enter into a relationship with him that

is personal, it is like going to a water park on a hot day. He brings cool refreshing water; it is enough to swim, splash and delight in. It is ok to have fun with God. There is enough of the Holy Spirit to fill, overflow and swim in. He wants to play with us like a father plays with his children at the amusement park. He delights in us; we need to recognize it and start delighting in him. A lot of times, we think God is only for serious conversations. No, he wants to be for fun, too.

In the dream, I am wearing my swim suit, but it is a park filled with snow. The snow symbolizes the forgiveness that Jesus offers through his blood according to Isa 1. 18. We, do not, however, need to wear clothes to his party, he has supplied them to us. We wear the robe of his righteousness through Jesus Christ. He wants us to come in our bathing suit (actually, naked; it's a skin party) and play in his snow; to delight in his forgiveness.

He wants us to have fun with him as our husband. He has come to release us from burdens, but we still do not let go. He has his arms extended to take our burdens and sins, but we still hang onto them. Then, they steal our delight. Only when we let go of our burdens, will be begin to delight in him.

Sometimes, we put ourselves into a place where we do not belong. He will call us back to the place where he wants us to be. In the dream, I go out on a ledge and my husband calls me back to a better way. The way that he calls me to has a slide. God wants to give us his 'slide'. He has provided a slide into his way of forgiveness.

When we try to conjure up our own joy; our own fun in the 'God realm' we will not be able to do it. We find ourselves out on a limb without no firm standing. We can stand with him, when we slip into what he has for us.

Then, in the dream, there is thunder and people leave the water park. The thunder is the word of God. When God showed up in the Old Testament on the Mountain with Moses and he spoke, the people thought it was thunder. They were frightened and ran. When God speaks to us, sometimes we become frightened and run. Why?

Maybe we are anticipating what he is going to say, and think that he will tell us that we are doomed. That is what the Children of Israel thought. They were frightened and told Moses to go forward for them and come back to tell them what God has to say. In Exodus, we can read how Moses, then ascends to the mountain and talks with God as a man talks to a man; face to face.

God wants to talk to each of us face to face, not just a select few. We need to ask him to change the fear of him that we have for a healthy one. If we are his children, then we can quickly claim grace and mercy, then run to his presence because we hide behind the face of Jesus when we are in his face. Jesus stands between us and God when we are in His presence 'through Christ', so we do not have to run. If we are running from the voice of God, then there are issues that we are refusing to deal with and we are afraid that he will reveal them to us. He already knows about them. He is God and knows everything.

I have a friend who converted from Buddhism. When she first started praying, she addressed God this way, "Dear God, This is Sarah, I am in Las Vegas (then she gave her address)."

I showed her Psalm 139 and how God knows her intimately. He knit her in the womb of her mother and continues to multiply every cell of her body up to now. Just like God knows everything about us, he also knows what we struggle with. He will be there to take it from us as we turn it over. We need to ask Him for the grace to do it.

When we go to the center; the center of where we are supposed to be, then what we have left will not be there. All of the cares that we have left at the foot of the Cross will be taken care of when we turn them over to Jesus. He only leaves a towel and a stethoscope.

The towel is for washing each other's feet. We are to enter into a ministry of serving each other as Jesus serves us.

Jesus showed the full extent of his love when he took off his outer clothing. He bared himself and wrapped himself in what was needed to serve others. He put aside his needs and adorned himself with what was needed to serve others needs. He poured himself out; shared his pure heart, and allowed it to become full of the dirt of the feet of the disciples. He allowed the road dirt, the evidence of life in this sinful world to taint his cleanness. He allowed his robe of righteousness to become the cleaning rag for their feet. They were made clean by his display of a servant. We need to have a cleansed preparation for preaching the Gospel.

Our feet need to be washed by his righteousness. Our preparation for service in the Kingdom of God is in caring for the needs of those that need to be served. Jesus brought himself, the water of his presence, the basin (emptiness before God), openness before the men (he disrobed), and a towel. He brought the towel. He didn't just leave them wet, he brought the provision for righteousness completed. He took away the water with his towel because he brought his presence; the Presence of God. There is no more reason for us to be thirsty because he has brought the water to us; we can be satiated. He came when we were thirsty and dirty and left us filled and clean.

Mary anointed the feet of Jesus before his burial by breaking a jar of expensive perfume and pouring it on his feet then cleansing them with her tears and wiping them with her hair. She poured out her soul to him. She was willing to share her inner emotions and expend herself for what she knew was right and he commended her for it. Her towel was her hair. Hair is adornment. She made only a thread between her and Jesus and cushioned it with her tears. She new truly who he was and wasn't afraid of what others thought of her. She knew he came to die for her sins was demonstrating her gratefulness to him for his sacrifice. She poured forth her fragrance. Her aroma filled the air. Our aroma fills whatever area that God has placed us in. We need not fear where he has placed us. Maybe there will be those who won't understand the intimacy of our relationship with Jesus, but they will respect it when they see our genuineness of heart and servant's attitude toward them.

A stethoscope is an instrument that is used by nurses and doctors for listening to our hearts to tell what kind of condition it is in. They can tell if it is functioning well. They can tell if it is sick.

In the Dream, the stethoscope is without the 'ear pieces'. It is impossible for a nurse to listen to someone's heart without that piece of the stethoscope. A stethoscope is made of a bell, and two tubes that echo the noise of the sounds to two ear pieces that fit into the ears. The enable the person to hear the heart of the one that they are listening to. In the dream there is no ear pieces. The message from God is that we are not supposed to listen to each other's hearts. It has not been given to us to know one another's heart condition before God. This is his job alone, not ours.

He is the one that weighs the hearts of men. He is the one that has the ability to speak directly to the heart. It is not us. We are not to judge other's conditions. We are not to assume the role of the physician in diagnosing each other's conditions. We need to leave it to the Great Physician. In fact, God says, that we are not even supposed to judge our own hearts. We are to give them into his hand and let him judge us. The true judge of our heart is the praise that we receive from God. When he says to us, "Well done, Good and faithful servant."

At any time we can ask God to test our hearts. He doesn't mend hearts, he makes them new. He is not interested in fixing what we have messed up. He wants to create in us a new heart.

II Chronicles 6.30, Nehemiah 13.14, Psalms 7.9, 27.21, 51, Proverbs 16.2, Ecclesiastes 2.10, Isaiah 25, Jeremiah 17, Zephaniah 3, Romans 8, I Corinthians 4.5, John 12,13, Revelation 7.17, 21.4.

Tremendous Fellowship

Let God arise in us to do His will through our lives, to birth His plans. Jesus send us a baby Announcement: I need to plan an private party. Begin preparations, set things out, plan ahead, ask for Him to show me where I am going. A party, apart with God alone, together, beside. Tremendous fellowship.

Passwich Sandwich

Become passwich
Be sandwiched between His
bread. Meet him.
Between the Old and the New,
Then and now.
Lettuce get together.
Meet.

By pass of the Father

We have all endured the enemy way too long getting in between us and God.
For God will be our by pass. Take notice when He comes. For, He passes
by and shines His light onto the screen of our subconscious spirit.
He shines his light on the backdrop of our soul. If we follow the
light. We can catch what we see in the sieve, for it is
ours to keep. Like pouring flour through a sifter,
His word comes and sifts down through the
screen. We get what is left.
Then, separate the eggs;
White from the yokes.
Purity of His presence
From the wiles of the
Devil. As we continue to
invite Him into our lives,
He will become as familiar as a friend.
If we continue to pursue the relationship, He will
pass by often.
We can cleaned out a room at our house and invite Him to stay.
Because He can will live with us, now through the provision
of the Holy Spirit. Our house has become His. No more
just a passing friend. When we have invited Him in
to stay. He has already adopted us, we need to
adopt Him. Like father and child.
There will be commitment and security.
He will
become both,
our father and our friend.

Two AM Conversation

It's a 2 AM conversation
with the 1 I love.
Hearts melted and met.
He pages me,
and I put Him on it.

His Faithful Page

Be embossed and enveloped. Be my
paper to become embossed with my stamp.
Be my page to become enveloped by my presence.
A page sent from a King to a kingdom's people
to be delivered one at a time
A letter on the doorstep
Special delivery
Postmarked
from
above
from the
Savior to serve
brought by His faithful page.

Three Companies

He said He was from three different companies
to turn me from a watcher into a real doer in the last time.
He pages me and I put Him on it.

God's Heart Flutter

Caterpillar spins the Cocoon. Not forever, but for a season.
We toil and spin for our season, but soon we will
burst forth with our new wings and fly.
Oh winged one
Fly.
Soar,
Oh, beautiful.
My heart flutters
as you fly. When you fly
where I send you
it's like a
hummingbird goes
from flower to flower.
I gasp with delight, glee.
You make your God to have glee
And delight to let me provide you with
my flowers. Mine have suckle for you to suck
the nectar from.
And, I will lounge on the porch swing and watch.
And you were afraid I wouldn't notice.
I Planted the flowers, and raised the hummingbird,
Why wouldn't I notice when they matched?
Drink the pollen , and spread the rest.
Be like a bee, be my honey.
Be like a bird, sing.
Sing of My honey, My sweetness,
My intimacy, The unity of your mouth
With My sweet flowers. Suckle the nectar
to deliver it somewhere else. Be My Bee. Be Mine.

Hummers

Humming birds hum when they draw from the flowers.
Why are you suppressed when you hum, as you
draw from Me?
You're a big Hummer.

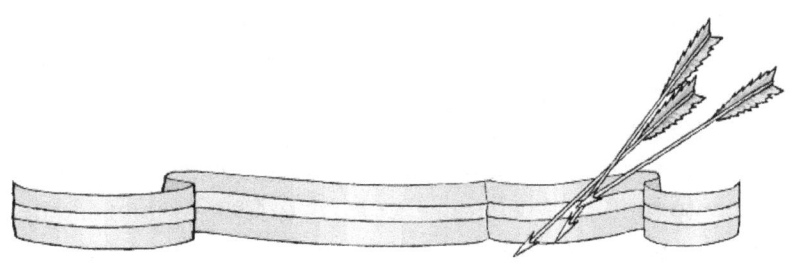

Chapter 5
John 14-16 Merge

Shadows

Sometimes we will have notions that dart in and out of our mind. They can keep us from focusing on what God has for us. We need to seek His protection for our focus to keep it on what He has for us. We can't mix our own notions with what God wants to build in our lives.

It is OK to be in love with God. He is in love with us already. We can not out love Him, but it is fun to try. We cannot give more of ourselves to Him than He has already given to us. The more of ourselves we give to Him, the more He will give of Himself.

We walk in His shadow. He leads us holding onto our hand like a father. The Son leads the way. He is the door of provision to the relationship with the Father. As the Son shines on the Father, we can walk in his shadow. As long as there is daylight, he has promised to hold onto our hand and lead us. He will show us the way we are to go. To some the shadow may seem frightening because the presence of God is so close. You can smell him; his cologne. He's not taller than us, he is at eye level with each one of us. He becomes to each of us as he desires.

Sometimes the shadow may seem like nighttime. We feel that God is not there and is not listening to our prayers. It is when the shadow is deepest. There are different depths to shadows depending on the size of the object that is causing the shadow. A feathery tree makes a light shadow, whereas a mountain makes a heavy shadow. We may feel nothing but heaviness in our life; perhaps we are going through a deep trial. God calls us to seek him with a new depth. Press in until we find him.

He says that he is never far from us. He is always near. He will continue to be that shadow for us. We need only to reach out. So, no matter how deep the shadow, he is always at the other side of it. He will stand between what blinds us. He will be our sunglasses to see the trials the world brings to us. He will always interpret the messages of the world if we bring them to him. Scarcely our feet leave to look for him and he is already there for us. He only wants us to take a step in his direction, and he will do the rest.

He comes to us out of the deep darkness that we live in. We are used to the darkness and are surprised when he shows up. He is laden with all kinds of gifts for us. He brings them from his storehouse. They have been there since eternity past waiting for us to sign for the delivery. Each one of us has a box waiting on the door step of our house. We need to sign for it, open the door and bring it inside to open it. Only inside of the love of God, can we open the box that contains the gifts that he has given us.

Song of Solomon

Who am I?

Where is my wallet? I have lost my identity.
I bet it's in His pocket hanging in the closet.
When I go there, I will find it. Go to Him in prayer.
Find out who I am, in Him.

Topeka, Kansas

Topeka Kansas is nowhere to me
But, somewhere to someone.
The place where you are
Is important to your Father.
And He can work just fine from the
middle of no where in places like Topeka, Kansas.

God's High School Tests

In this High School Class, these tests come
with instructions enclosed. And there is a tutor.
He's not a proctor, but a close friend that permits
us to peek over his hand to copy the answers.
If we wear our glasses and face the right
direction, we will be able to see all
the answers. There is no reason
why we shouldn't come
out with an A.
The
problem with a test is that it is multiple choice.
There is always one definite wrong choice.
You can immediately discount, but
Then, the questioning starts.
For, you find yourself
wedged between
Good, better
and
best.
It becomes
a matter of perspective.
That is when we need
to start thinking from
the perspective
of the instructor, wisdom.

Open Book Test

There are take home tests. Usually, they take a long time,
but can be done with an open book.
Almost always, however, you can get a favorable score
because, the book is poured over by the one doing the test.

Challenge

God gives challenge to the weary.
Because, when we are tired, then we need help.
And,
when
we need
help, we
call out to Him.
The challenge is that
how soon we will cry out.
Do we wait until we are at a complete loss as to what to do,
Or do we call out sooner, in the situation? The kingdom
of God is not advanced by our courage, our stamina,
or our ability. There is a critical point where
our endurance stops and His starts; where we
can't do it any longer. We need Him. We
have reached a place where there is none of us.
Do we lay down, give it up, submit to the devil?
His trick is to come up from behind us and tell us to pull
ourselves up by using others. We need help.
So, we ask others to assist us. This
is wrong. God says that
He is the one who
supplies our
needs.
Not others. So, the test comes when we are spent,
only then, can He push us to a new level calling on
His grace. We don't call on the grace of people.
Get behind us, Satan, for you are a tricker,
and we call on the grace of God, now
to help us. Father, we need
you. Become in us,
whatever we
need to get Your job
done. Then, we put our head
down, like a blocker on a football team,
and push through. While He tests our endurance.

Open Book Life

Our Life is to be an open book. Others take us home
as they see us go through test after test and pass.
Usually, there is a favorable outcome.
Because, when they see us turn to our book for
the answers; Keep it open by memorizing it and
placarding it around our life, then, we appear
to come
up with the right
answers on a pretty reliable basis.
It's about the long term relationships we
have with others. They watch God test
us, then stand by as a proctor ready
with their
red pen and
their stars to see
how we do. *I wonder,*
sometimes, if they think we cheat
by always leaving the answer book open?

Let's be Mine

Be still and know that I am God.
When you are still,
and you let Me talk to you,
all will know who I Am.
I own the quietness, when I own you.
It's mine as you are Mine. Let's be Mine.

Neon Freeway Sign

The best sign to have on the free way is programmable from off site and neon. Be flexible to have the words flow and change. Be electrified by the Holy Spirit. Stand up and shout, "This is the way!" Billboards are put on main roads, freeways. Becoming a big sign means that God will position you in the field, plaster His message on you, Then turn on the power. Remember, your light doesn't change. But, the darker it gets, the more you will be seen.

Dependency

Dependency is a God thing
when what you are
depending on doesn't depend on
anything else.

Glowing Embers

Twirling, spinning, setting afire
Glowing embers.
Glowing embers, igniting vision.
Eyes glowing around the bon fire.
Look at Him
Be a glow

Climb the Mountain

When you are obedient to the vision that God has put in your heart, then, you can say that you gave it your all, So, they can say 'thanks'. The mountain climb will be worth the effort when you reach the peak and look out on all that God has given you. Become a mountain climber for Him. Climb to that Place within His presence that reaches to the height of His vision.

God's Transportation System

It's not a matter of research
how we take from one pile and give to another.
It's a matter of being willing to become part of the
transportation system of God's love.

Let Him Push

He is not our voice, But the air behind it. Let Him
push on your diaphragm. Let Him press on you, uplift you, up lift
your voice as you lift up His.

Pass the Shuttle

We are woven like on a loom.
He moves us one way, then passes the shuttle.
Then He moves us another way, then passes it again.
I can feel Him within. He doesn't constrict or restrict.
But He rewrites the main points
then threads us
through
the
middle
of them.
He changes our desires.
This is my desire to honor you from the inside out
You become shown to others as you are on My Inside
Then, we learn to become transparent to others.
Then they see Christ in us, the hope of glory.

Waiting on God

The Dream:
My husband and I are in a car stuck in a Drive-through behind a white car. No one is behind us, but there is a definite flow direction and going backwards is not an option. There is a hold-up and we get bored. We have a lot of money, so we get out of the car and play money games in the street between the white car and us. Then the car starts to move and we abort the money and hop in the car. We tailgate the white car to make it through the turnstiles and gates to the other side. We try to go back for the money, but a gray van comes screeching up and three guys jump out and take the money. We don't care because we don't need the money.

Interpretation:
The white car represents the righteousness of God and his leading in

our lives. There is only one-way to drive through this relationship with him. Sometimes he tells us to wait on him. The waiting is an active process, however.

In the dream I am bored. This mean two things. It could mean that there is a loss of interest in the direction that he wants us to go, or that we become 'bored' through by his word as it is etched on our heart.

As we wait on him, we are supposed to lay down our own provisions, my payment for the settlement of our own debts. It is 'big money' according to the world, but it is street trash is God's eyes. We are to lay it down between him and us openly on the pavement for all to see. We should lay down the sacrifices of our own hands, our righteous acts, our plans, our trust in money, our past, our sins, and our afflictions.

He waits patiently for us like he waited for Noah to build the Ark. It should not have taken so many years for Noah to build that Ark. God could not let it rain on the earth until the Ark was built. So, he waited on Noah to become ready.

Just like Noah, for us, He needs a vessel ready to weather the storm. We need to learn to wait on him. To listen for his voice, watch for his hand in our life, set ourselves to learn his heart's desire. Drink from the water of his Holy Spirit. He has appointed a harvest in our lives. The vision will come because he is faithful.

Proverbs 8, Psalms 40, 130, Isaiah 43, 62, 64, 65, Hosea 6, Habakkuk 2:3, Lamentations 3:22, James 5, I Peter 3: 20.

Imprint

Is it about seeing my name in print or
seeing His imprint?

Order of God

Words: *We can't look over the menu of God's righteousness. We must take what he gives for food. He will order for us. It will be brought.*

Interpretation:
We can't pick and choose from God's righteous orders for our life. He has orders already. He will bring them at just the right time; a course at a time.

God wants to display his righteousness in our life. He has a completed menu of righteousness, but will only bring certain things at a time. God serves us. He waits on us to be ready for our order of spiritual food. When he provides us with the heavenly food, it brings 'order' to our messed up life.

There are different kinds of eaters. There are hungry eaters; those that are starved for the words of God and eat everything on their plates quickly. They eat all he has put before them and ask for 'seconds'.

There are 'big eaters'. Those with high energy and can consume a lot at one sitting. They might read large sections of scripture or spend hours in prayer. They desire to turn up the volume of God's word to their lives.

There are 'picky eaters. These are those who hear the words of God and doubt it. They might hear a small voice in their spirit telling them to do something, but they pick at it until they no longer believe it is from God. These allow doubt to creep in and steal the words that God has for them. They continue to ask, "is this God's voice?' until they don't believe that God is speaking to them at all. Sometimes we keep sending the food back to the kitchen because we do not like it. Maybe we do not like the words that God is telling us. Or maybe we ignore the peas and eat the bread. God has given us both, but we choose not to listen to the whole message. Do we send the food back to the kitchen because we didn't order it that way? If God's orders come to us in a way we didn't order, do we refuse them?

A course is the direction of progress or the path over which something moves. It is a sequence of travel; a flow. A course can also be a term used to denote a specific instruction given for a purpose to an outcome. It leads to advancement in that area of study.

God longs for our righteousness to be made complete. But we move from one level to another. Glory to glory. The courses from God are on righteousness. We move through the levels of his righteousness. We become the righteousness of Jesus through us as we move closer to God through his course. Each course has waters of desire, bread of presence, milk of longing for him, obedience through the meeting, and if we hang out long enough; he will light the candles (fire of God) and we will linger with his wine, the delight. When the work is done, the course is complete, then we will have wine together.

We cannot order our courses from God. When we finish one course of our 'meal' he will bring the next one. We have to finish the course of 'salad' before he will bring the course of 'main meal'. He waits on us to eat what he has set before us. When we finish the whole course, down to the garnish, then he will bring us the next one.

When God brings us our course, and sets it before us, what do we do with it? Do we refuse it and send it back? Do we throw it away? Do we take only what we want and leave the rest to others?

We need to take whatever he sets before us and eat. We don't pick God's plan for our life. The plan has been set before the earth was created. We may make plans, but His is the one with the guarantee because His power backs His plan.

He has placed the desires for the Kingdom of God and the 'place setting' on our tables. The desires for his kingdom have already been placed in our hearts as part of his plan within creation. The place setting is before us. We all have a place within the kingdom of God. The dishes need to be emptied. We must empty ourselves out of our own plans. He has not called us to 'work in the kitchen' for our meal. He does not want us to get to his goals by works.

We have to empty our hands, make them available for his use before he can put into them the tools to deal with the course that he needs to set before us on our table. If we are too busy hanging onto what we have already ordered, then there is not room on the table for his order. If we are so full of our own orders 'full of ourselves', there will be no hunger in our hearts for the real food that comes from him.

It is God's plan for Him to wait on us. He waits on us because He will not cram food down our throat; He will not force his will on us.

It is His nature to wait on us because it is His nature to serve us. Even Jesus came not to be served, but to serve and to give his life as a ransom for many.

Proverbs 15.21, Psalms 19.5, I Corinthians 9.24, Galatians 2.2, 5.7, Philippians 2.16, Hebrews 12.1,5.10, James 3.6.

Three Fold Wrap

When there's a three fold wrap, an intertwining
of love to love with the Father, Holy Spirit and
me, it doesn't matter how loose the twine is,
it is strong. It works no
matter what.
Sometimes, I look at
others and think that they don't
love God enough. But, He
says that if they love,
it is enough to
make it work
because
then
He can
make twine so
that the vine can grow
up the trellis. Only, when the
relationship is close, then the intertwining
becomes rope. It can be used to rescue others.

Buying Righteousness

Dream:
I was sent to buy underwear for a big woman. There was none. I could only find a fake fur fluorescent girdle. They came in several fluorescent colors.
Words: *No righteousness can be bought. None is available.*

Interpretation:
We are to be light, not bright. There is a difference between bright and light. Bright has loud color that tries to be noticed. Light does not. God wants us to be light, not bright. He does not call on our own brightness (our own mental attentiveness), but to be reflection of His lightness.

Believe in or not, there are girdles in Bible. There were girdles given to the first priests when the Nation of Israel was formed. It was an undergarment that Aaron, Moses' brother wore when he was set apart as a priest for the people. It was part of the ceremonial garb that he wore. The girdle of Aaron was of finely twisted linen the colors of gold, blue, purple and scarlet yarn. As Aaron wore the girdle, he also wore a turban that was engraved with a seal "Holy to the Lord".

There was a specifically prescribed ceremony that Moses led when the priests were set apart for the service of God. After they became consecrated, then they could offer sacrifices for the people for their sins. The climax of the celebration was when God showed up with his presence. It was what they had all waited for. When all the people saw it they shouted for joy and fell face down.

Jesus has a girdle, too. His is the symbolic wrap of his righteousness. His righteousness wraps around everything he does and is. When we join with him, then he wraps this girdle around us.

We need to be careful of those who tell us to purchase our own girdle. Our girdle is what provides our right standing before God.

We have nothing to buy our righteousness with because we are completely sinful. We have been born into sin and the only hope of us having any purity is through the blood of Jesus.

The dream tells us that if we try to buy our own way to heaven, it may look colorful, even fluorescent, but will not support us at the door.

Jesus calls us his sheep. He wants to give us white wool, purity in following him as part of the flock. In the dream, I find fake fur. There is only fake fur, or faux, (the fox comes alive) at the store that I go to. The door to the store that the real fur is sold at is only opened through the blood of Jesus. He is the only way to righteousness that will bring us into right standing with the Father. There is no other way whereby men can be saved. If anyone comes to us with any other girdle, tell them to keep it.

Faces of God

Words:
I have many faces (of God). I show different healings by my different Spirits. I bring healing 7 ways.

Jesus came to the earth and reflected the very face of God. His face shines with the radiance of God in all his Glory. It shines like the sun with all the brilliance of the creator of the Earth because he was. God showed his face to man through him.

When Jesus went to Heaven, he gave us the Holy Spirit, who also reflects the face of God to us. The Holy Spirit reflects his face through us, however, not to us. When his face shines upon us he fills our heart with everything that he is. Because God can write on our heart, he leaves an impression on us just like the plates that print money. We become the working surface of what ever he wants to give to others of himself. It provides the front side to make others see his mind. His mind is brought forward to the world through us.

The peace of God overflows from the heart onto the face. Then all of the attributes of God come out in our lives. We must see his face before we can reflect it. We have to get close enough to feel his breath on our neck. We see him with our heart.

He writes his messages on our hearts of what he wants his face to reveal about his character. Through his power and grace, being dependent on him, we have become competent messengers of the gospel. It is an eternal message given to all. Some may find this message (glow) difficult to be near. Just like the Israelites could not look at the face of Moses because of the reflection of the glory, the same is true for us. Others may not be able to look at our face because it is too bright to them.

The face we need to show others is the true face of God. We are to comfort them with the comfort that he gives us when we face sufferings. In the face of despair, we offer his face of hope.

Following the way of love reflects the face of God to others.

We need to share our hearts with others to reveal his face to them. When we show that we are weak, it only shows how to depend on God. He has given us freedom to fail. He will uphold us amidst all.

Numbers 6.25, Psalms 4.6, 105.4, Song of Solomon 2.14, Isaiah 50.6, Matthew 17.2, I Corinthians 13.12, II Corinthians 2,3, 4, I Peter 3.12, Revelation 1.16, 22.4.

Feel the Power

You can feel the power as God works
through His people
to make them to become His desire.
As our desire is for Him,
He fulfills our desire.
As His desire is for us, we fulfill it.

Old Instruments of Computation

†
Add it up.
One life committed
to Him becomes multiplied
3 into 1. Body, soul, spirit into Him.
There will always be a trailing number of 3
God will continue to be magnified forever.
There are some old instruments that
need to be taken out of the place
where they have been left
neglected. They are
ancient,
old and dusty.
No one even knows how to play them any more.
How does that happen? Does the teacher die,
or do the students loose interest? Then,
someone learns to play one that has not
been played in a long time. People
will stare, stop and listen.
Sing bird,
sing for your love.
Live the love,
For the love is alive to live through you.
Open your mouth. Allow My Spirit to flow through you.
You have no idea what you sound like, what you look like,
What you smell like. The old name for gladiolus is flags. Be My
flag. Wave my fragrance. You are grown from My bulb planted
along the path to the road to holiness.

Building Ourselves

The Dream:
We try to do our own building and everything falls through. We build around the tree. The structure is like bamboo. It is flimsy.
Then we take the family to the sea. It is hard to get them into their suits. Everyone goes different directions. They are like taking toddlers to the beach. They spill their formula on each other.

Interpretation:
When we try to do our own building, everything falls through. We cannot build ourselves into what God wants us to be. We need to be built on him by taping into the tree, not building around it. He has not called us to abide 'near' him but 'in' him. It is risky to abide 'in' Christ. We must depend on the branches to be strong enough to handle our weight. We have to put our 'wait' on him instead of using our own timing. When we build our own structure, we will not know which materials to choose and the structure will not be able to hold up when there is bad weather or wind. It will be made of wrong stuff. Only God knows how to build sturdy, eternal structures, that last the tests of time.

We cannot take the family of God into the sea either. We cannot make them to see God for themselves. We cannot lay out suits for others to climb into. There is no way that providing a 'job' list for people to sign up on is going to work. Babies are born naked and that is the way God wants us to stay. He wants to provide the suit for us to swim in. He will bring us into seeing him, his way.

When we try to provide jobs for others to get them working in the Kingdom of God, then they will start to cooperate, but it will not work out. They will be like a bunch of toddlers trying to get into swim suits. Unless we stay with them every step of the way, they will not make it to the sea (seeing mode). Even if they cooperate for a while, their natural tendencies will kick in after while and they will veer off toward them. If we put someone into the 'song' ministry when God has a special job for them in the Children's' ministry, then they will become distracted with the children and be bad at the song leading. It does not work for us to try to dress one another. We will spill our formula on each other. The formula that we have for our own growth will not work for others because they are not in the same place.

It is like a map of the mall. We need to know where we are before we can get to the destination. We are each in different spots on the map of our journey to God. It will not help to coach someone else on the directions that God has given us individually, because the next person is starting out in a different place and going by an alternate route. We each must take our own trail to the Kingdom of God.

Can I have an Aaron?

I'm looking for an Aaron. For I sense how Moses felt.
Oh, to stand between a nation and a powerful God to be the one who hears His voice and passes the messages on; To see the fear in both of their eyes.
The people are afraid to get close.
Afraid of themselves. Afraid of their own sin.
Afraid of the unknown. And the Lord.
He, too, has fear in His eyes.
Fear of rejection. One more time, His word is shunned.
They come to the edge of the mountain, yet won't go up to the place of communion.
Somehow, I don't think Moses knew that he would have to face that big monster.
For, he panicked when he was to face the small one;
pharaoh. He asked his brother
and his brother went before him in Egypt.
And in the crossing of the Red Sea.
But, yet, his brother, didn't have what it took
to climb the mountain and face God.
He was invited. They all were.
But, for Moses, he knew the heart of God,
that the rumbles of thunder were merely a display
of the excitement and anticipation of Him meeting
at an intimate level with one He loved.
Of course, he would go.
And, he loved to go alone.
For, then, he didn't have to share God with others.

I think, he thought he needed Aaron,
but when it came right down to the real mission,
Aaron was not prepared, did not go,
and was left at the foot of the mountain.
Sometimes I think I need an Aaron
to join me when God gives me a hard job.
I pick someone, convince them to join my cause,
and train him to be just like me.
I tell him everything I know to prepare him.
Then, I put him out front as a pad
between me and the situation God wants to put me into.
It doesn't work
because God trains each of us individually
for what He calls us to do.
Our training is a combination of our past experiences,
and learning to hear His voice for direction.
He puts us through experiences,
then leads us through to victory.
We become trained, tested and purified.
We learn the right answer through repetition.
He starts out with something little and works on up
the ladder of our training, progressing
to the larger mission of our life.
So, that when we finally reach our final mission,
we will be prepared by his school of Higher learning.
So, if we put someone in front of us, it won't work.
He will stumble, we will fall on him
and God's purpose will be faltering.
Leading by God is leading, not pushing.
He does not approve of us pushing others into our calling, pretending
that it is their leading.
He has one of their own.
So, if he is busy doing ours, who will do his?
Aaron got caught up making the golden calf
for the Children of Israel because he was not prepared to lead them by
God's training in the desert like his brother.
Moses placed him in a position that he wasn't ready for, and it hurt
many. We should learn a lesson from them.

On, second thought, I don't think I want an Aaron, God.
Please, give me the grace I need to do what you tell me to do, when you tell me to do it, and in Your time.

Spin Out

The dream:
I am in a car. We are following a fire truck. My father is in the front seat along with my brother. I am in the back seat behind my father in a small sedan car. My father is in the driver's seat, but I am driving the car. We all have steering wheels. I don't have any pedals for gas and brake, but I have an emergency brake. The road is windy and it is dark out. I can barely see over my father in the front seat. I loose sight of the fire truck. All of a sudden there are some black trash bags in the roadway. I try to stop the car but loose control. I can't find the brakes. I hit them and we go into a complete spin and are ready to go over the steep embankment. I yell at my father in the front seat to steer the car from the front seat. Up until now, I didn't notice that He had a steering wheel. He and my brother have made no effort to drive up to this point. He has been sitting back with his arm over the seat. He comes to alertness and is ready to take the steering wheel. I continue to be scared and use my emergency brake to stop the car. I never give him an opportunity to drive because I panic and use the emergency brake before he drives the car.

Interpretation:
I am in charge of my own life. I am trying to run things on my own. I have put God into the driver's seat of my car (my life), but continue to steer by manipulation from the back seat.

When I pray, because I know the Word of God, I contend with God, thinking that I already know the outcome. The Holy Spirit will not take control if we are controlling the program. The fire engine relates to someone going to a fire. I am seeking the 'fire of God' and going in the right general direction. But when I do not rely upon the Holy Spirit for everything, my own trash gets in the way. I cannot see into the darkness with my physical eyes, therefore I need spiritual eyes to direct me.

My pride told me that I could see 'over' my father into the path that the car was going to go. Darkness overwhelmed me and I spun out. The only control that was left was the emergency brake, which is my will to 'stop'. God does not take our free will from us. He does not grab control in our life when we loose control because our own will, pride, trash, and spiritual blindness that causes us to spin out of control. He will not tolerate us doing ministry in His Kingdom by manipulation from the back seat, either. He desires for us to turn over freely the control of the ministry in our lives to Him. He needs to drive us. Our only recourse is to be driven by Him, or put on the emergency brake (bail out of it altogether). I am not in the right position to see the road clearly, and to steer clear to the trash ahead. I have put myself above my brothers and my Father (Pride and Idolatry of self) thinking that I could control the whole car from the back seat. When I try to drive from the back seat, I cannot do it, will spin, crash and cause the destruction of the whole carload.

In the dream, the father doesn't have a brake in the front seat, I only have an emergency brake. In true, God doesn't have a brake, because He always longs to pursue a relationship with us, it is we who brake from Him, often when our life gets out of control and we don't turn the wheel over to Him. I cannot take His plan and my own heart. I have to allow Him to control my heart. Only God's love can drive me, nothing else, or I am found to be in the driver's seat by manipulation.

If I have been given the heart of God, How do I let God's heart drive me? Let go of the wheel, ask for help, trust in His Word, listen to His Voice, obey. Notice that the father never jumped out of the car, even when it was spinning out of control. He just waited on me. He never leaves us. What I need to do is give up 'my vision' for God's Vision. Only He can see the road. A spirit of hypocrisy, self indulgence and uncleanness compels me to think that I am worthy to drive the car above my Father or my brother, even though they are both in the front seat and have steering wheels.

Job 32.8, 32.19, 36.16, Psalms 119, Isaiah 51, II Corinthians 5:14.

Prophecy Clause

When God has a mission for us, He will tell us. Not someone else, to tell us. He is a personal God who speaks to individuals. We need to question messages that come from others, checking to see if they are from God.

Sometimes, He will confirm a message that He has already given to you through a message from someone else. That's OK. But, when someone comes to you with a new message, you should question it. God does not mind being questioned. He is happy to answer our questions. If the message is not for you, and you start to take it as your own, it will throw you onto another train track going a different direction than you should be going. Then, you will have problems when you end up in another city, unprepared to handle the climate there. And, that person who gave you the message.

What happened there? Sometimes when God gives us a message for our lives, we get so excited, that it spills over into everything we do. And, we start to think that our message, our purpose, our ministry is for everyone. So, like children on a playground, when we see an eligible team mate, we tag him for our side.

We need to remember that it is God that sends people, not us. For, when we send people to do what God has not authorized, then they will end up in another city without baggage. And they are not on the train they are supposed to be on. Their original intention has been abandoned because they are seeking your intention, instead of the Lord's.

So, every message, every 'word from God' given by someone with the gift of prophecy comes with a clause. *'Only follow these words if they are confirmed by God, Himself.'*

Peeping Toms

Peeping Toms look through windows they are not authorized to look through. What are they looking for? A life they don't have, circumstances the have not been given. But, why do they do it? The want what they think will never be theirs. They try to visualize their dreams through other's lives. I think my name might be Tom.

Cracking Walnuts

Walnuts are the biggest nut there is.
You can't crush a walnut in your hand.
What makes   you think
  you can crack some of the big nuts
  Around you with your bare hands.
     This lesson isn't very deep.

Stealing Uniforms

Dream :
I am with a friend. We are on an empty bus and he steals some clothes out of someone's bag. They belong to a tall basketball player and will never fit him, but he steals them anyway. I say nothing.

Then we go into a garage and hide in the upper storage area. We watch people come to the house for a party while we hide. After a while, I get hungry and climb down from the garage. I go to the house where there are people having a party.

Interpretation:
We are on an empty bus. It is a means of transporting a lot of people to the same place. There are several seats where each person sits in their own seat while the driver takes them all to one place. Our movement toward Heaven is like we are on a bus. The Church should be moving together in the same direction . Each of us should assume the position that God as assigned to us. Then we take our seats, look toward the front and leave the driving to God.

In the dream, the bus is empty because we are not taking our proper places using the transportation he has provided for us. It a bus that transports a team. The Church is to work as a team with the unified goal of bringing as many to salvation and victory as possible.

Like a 'high' School basket ball team, God has uniforms for us to wear. He wants to be our tailor, to fit us for the attire that is perfect for us. It is the right size in every direction for the position that he has for us to play as part of the team. On a football team, the kicker wears a different uniform than a fullback. He has special shoes whereas the fullback has special padding in certain places. They are each part of the team, but their attire is different.

God wants to give us special attire for the job within the Kingdom of God that he has prepared for us. If he wants us to be a writer, then he would dress us with provisions of computer skills, advanced education, and, perhaps, creativity in a certain direction. If he wants us to become an evangelist, he may give us a uniform with 'speaking skills' in our background. He longs to steer us down his path, his direction toward his goal. We need to pay attention to his voice for the directives.

In the dream, the friend takes someone else's uniform. It does not fit. When we try to be someone that we are not, it does not fit. It won't fit our personality. It is not what we are meant to do within the Kingdom. It is just like a short person trying to wear a basketball uniform. Just because he puts on the uniform, does not mean that he will be able to play on the team in the same position that the other person plays. We are not to follow in each other's footsteps, but in God's footsteps. Others can not teach us because our position is different. God has made us individual, just like snowflakes. None of us is alike. We may be similar, but not alike.

When we assume the position that God has intended for us, we become a tool to be used in his hand. In the dream, we become tools that are stored. We store tools when it is 'off season'. When we don't need the skis, we store them. When we don't need the rake or the hoe, we store them. Because my and my friend have taken a uniform that was not ours, it does not fit. When we put on attire that belongs to someone else, we will be out of place. We will feel out of season because we will be out of season. Nothing will feel right. If our gifting is in the area of music, and we are trying to wear a 'uniform' of helping with Children's ministries, then it is like wearing a uniform that is not made for us. We will feel out of season because we will be out of touch with the season. It is not for us. The true person will go into hiding behind the 'mask' of the other uniform. God cannot use us when we are not true to ourselves and him.

When we do what God intends for us to do, it will satisfy us. We will not be satisfied, we will continue to be hungry for what his intended will for us is until it comes to happen. God places the hunger in our 'bosom' to fulfill the mission that he has planned for us. He will make us hungry to see that vision fulfilled. We will remain hungry, even though we may be very busy, when we are not doing his intended mission for us. He wants to satisfy us by bringing us into his house and feeding us with his vision and direction.

Deuteronomy 7.6-8, Psalms 18, II Corinthians 5.11-21, I Peter 1.13-22, Ephesians 5:8-10.

Gold Dust

Salvation wasn't our idea.
Why do we build on our own ideas now?
We defile what is pure with our own dust because
we are made of dust. God has provided us
with access to His Wisdom, Knowledge,
Understanding and Revelation.
He has given us the keys
to the Kingdom.
He gives us
gold dust
that
can
be
made into whatever
He chooses. His ideas are
eternal and priceless. When, we follow
His plan for His ideas, we build into His desire.

Half a bridge

Complication arises when we start
Out with God's plan and finish
with
ours.
It is like building a bridge
half way from either side
with a different plan.
They don't meet up
very smoothly
in the
center
to allow the
vision to cross over.

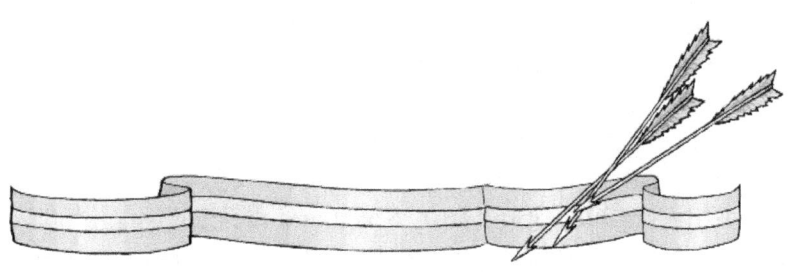

Chapter 6
Growing Service

The Spirit of Might Flows

The power of God is by the flow of the Holy Spirit. He does not give his Spirit by measure. If we have the Holy Spirit, we have all of him. There is no such thing as 'part of the gifts of God'. God does not give us part of himself. If we have the Holy Spirit indwelling us, then at any time, he can raise up any spiritual gift that he wants.

The Might is the force; the press. It is the degree of pressure as from a valve. It is like a valve that releases the gas into the engine to make more power. The potential for the release is always there, but the valve needs to be opened to release it.

The valve needs to be turned sideways to open up for the might to be released. It is like we are the valve in the engine. We stand between the flow of the power (Holy Spirit) and the output to the engine to make the car run faster. The total power of God is available at any time, but it is released through our ministry; through us. It is as if we are the very hands of God reaching out to the world.

To release the Spirit of Might we need to become an obedient valve. We need to lay down. We need to flatten, like a lever that allows the gas to flow into the engine as it runs faster and faster.

We need to turn our heart toward Him and open up at both ends. We need to open up to God, then open up to others. What ever area of service he has put us in, he wants the Spirit of Might to flow through.

It is where the miracles happen. It is like when the wing is pulled in toward the F14, it decreases the drag and the jet flies faster with more power. The power was always there, but had not been released because the flaps were in the way. We must become flat before God. Flatten ourselves. We are in the way of the release of the power; Might. Our valves are stuck. They are gunked over with our own grime. We need to use soap and a brush.

The soap is the bubbles of the Holy Spirit and the cleansing blood of Jesus. The brush is to be used to paint the picture that God wants us to 'walk into.'

Service Season

The Dream:

I dreamt that I woke up and my alarm clock wasn't there on the night stand. I knew that I needed to get up for work at 0530 AM and was concerned that I would be late for work if I didn't get up on time, so I asked my husband about it. He said that He didn't have it.

I thought, "How will I know the time?"

God said, "You will know. Service Season will come, you will know it."

Interpretation:

We need to go through steps to get ready for His service. Often, we are in service, but not His service. We are serving ourselves, and others doing what we think He wants us to do, instead of going directly to the Captain for orders. He wants us to come directly to Him for orders. He will purify us in the service by teaching us himself.

When we do a ministry selected not directed by God, we set ourselves us for crushing failure. We take on the 'burden' of the ministry instead of resting in God's arm chair. For instance, if we are in a praying ministry, we might pray for hours feeling that if we don't pray, God's will won't happen. We get into thinking that His will is dependent on us? We may feel that we can't take the chance of someone not turning to God because we are too busy sleeping to pray. This trap is one of 'works' based ministry. We can add nothing to the sacrifice of Jesus.

God desires us to confirm our 'calling' in Christ Jesus. We must forget what lies behind and press forward toward the mark for the upward call of God in Christ Jesus.' God himself only knows where that 'target' is.

God is not only a friend, but a refiner. He is like a refiner's fire or a launderer's soap to us. If we allow ourselves to be refined by him, then our offerings to him will be acceptable. When we seek the presence of God, we are standing in front of him. How can we think that we can stand in His presence without being refined? Surely there is sin in our lives that needs his soap.

We need to have an attitude of 'alarm'. It is a reality that we have an enemy that seeks to destroy us. We need to become aroused to determine if God had given us the ministry that we are presently embracing. We need to examine our motives.

We need to have a desire to make things right. A persistent craving for the things of God rather than the things of the world. We should long for the fruit that endures to eternal life. We need to be aroused to look and see if our goals are God's goals. If we find that we have run into a wall, then it is actually a ceiling. We have grown too tall for the area that we are in. God wants to move us. At this point we need to lay our goals down and allow God to rebuild His goals in us. The question is: What concerns God?

We must lay down our goals and asked Him for His. We should determine not to let the enemy have a foothold in our life: To take His Kingdom goals seriously instead of 'our own my' goals for others. We must set ourselves to listen to His voice better. Not only to speak, but to stop speaking when the Holy Spirit tells us to. Not only to walk when He says, 'walk', but to stop walking and turn; even pivot when He says to. If we walk by the Spirit, we should learn to get into step with him.

We need to respond to his rebuke with humility and seek Him in prayer, putting His goals forward instead of ours. When God wants to use someone in a big way, that person needs an extra dose of humility and neediness. We must determined that when God speaks to our heart, we will be the first on our knees, the first to the altar, and the first to repent. This shows the character God desires of a servant and leader.

God is leading his Church through a season. He longs to lead us to Passover into a place where we can bare His fruit of righteousness. He has a plan already set out. We are stars, lights that serve to mark the seasons. He has called us to be alert to His alarm, not our own alarm. He desires for us to listen to his voice as to when to set out and when to stay 'camped'. He has provided servants as messengers to deliver messages to his people that tell of the seasons.

Yet, we continue to sin by setting our own seasons, doing our own seasoning. However, He loves us so much, that He will continue to draw us back to him. He desires to take from us the Valley of Achor (trouble) and give us a door of hope. He has made a covenant is to build his church. Our ability to alter this covenant is about as much control as we have to alter the sun and the moon rotating around the earth with it's seasons. His covenant of peace and compassion yields fruit in his season when we become his seasoning.

Ecc 3:1-22, Dan 2:21, Num 9:1,10:1-10, Ps 104: 1-35, Hosea 2:9-23, Ps 1, Prov 8:1,10,15:23, Jeremiah 5:25, 33:15-26, Ez 34:20.

Beautiful Bloomers

Tulips bloom in the spring because they have been planted in the fall. It is The planting that activates the bulb. It goes from dormant to becoming a beautiful display of color and light. When we are planted in the garden of His love, we trade dormancy for a beautiful display of what He wants to raise us up to be. Beautiful bloomers, blessing our brothers, because we've been bought with the blood and believe it. Beautiful, blessed, Belief, between us.

True Purpose

We dwell in a world full of menial tasks longing to recognize eternal purpose. Bombarded with an overload of information that is useless, We strive to make sense out of our lives. Since He died, was buried, and rose, He has opened the door that provides the light needed to see greater purposes in our lives. He has not opened our eyes, but the eyes of our heart which brings about an understanding of the true meanings of life and purpose.

Impatient Call

I did not say, "Give to me and I will give to you."
I said, "Call to me and I will answer you."
You called, but never expected an answer.
My answer is coming.
But you wouldn't wait. You got impatient.

Rain Water in a Cup

A cup collects rain water as it drips off the corner of the tent. Why?
You can't drink from the lake.
The brook could be tainted, there is no chlorine tablets, and, the fire went out a long time ago.
How much water can be collected?
It depends on how big the tent is.
The bigger the canopy, the more rain can be gathered. And, when the cup gets full, it is poured into containers.
So, we ask God to cover us with His blessings.
They trickle down from heaven and gather on our tent. Then, they all migrate toward the place
where they will fill our cup.
Then what?
We pour those blessings into others lives.
There is a time in this process
when we will be staring at the bottom
of our blue speckled cup. Don't panic.
Just put it back under the place where the blessings flow.

(For more on this principle of overflowing with the gifts of the Holy Spirit into other's lives see *Sharing Prophetic Gifts in the Church*.)

Store Fronts

Why do we put store fronts on buildings? We want to project an image of bigness; importance, to the community to help sell our products. We entice them to buy what we offer. We don't care if they need it, for we just want to sell it. We aren't interested in a relationship, we merely want to make a living for ourselves. We put store fronts on ourselves as well. We project an image to others, afraid that the one behind it will not be adequate to sell us to them. We have sold ourselves short in the process. We hide behind what we think we need to become, rather than being honest with us both. What would our town look like if we took off all those fronts? What is inside each place would look the same. So, who are we fooling? Not others, and not ourselves. We are stalling from becoming what we need to be. Perhaps we just need a face lift. Jesus provides the lift to our chin, the smile to our eyes, the shine to our face, and the bounce to our step. And, He is happy to come in the open door of our heart. He doesn't care about store fronts. They just get in the way.

We are a Picture Puzzle

We are made complete through Him. That means if we don't come to Jesus and seek His way, then we remain unfinished. Like a puzzle with part of the pieces missing, the picture will never be completed to show others that picture of who God is.

Etched in Stone

Eloquent words, beautiful messages,
written in love, etched in stone.
Jesus the rock,
the Word to us.

Uphold Truth

Unless all of your action upholds
the belief of who
I really am,
Then by pass Me all together!
For, I do not need another sign
that points people in the wrong direction!

Invitation

Words: *I will feed them myself.*
The dream: God says, "I invite someone to dine with me. We go to the restaurant but the table is taken by a regular. I want to feed someone but the table is taken by a regular."

Interpretation:

The Lord wants us to dine with him. He has invited us to dine with Him at his table. He is waiting with his presence, but he needs a table.

What is the table? A surface where food is served. The food is the word of God as it is given to us. It is whatever he wants to tell us.

The table is our heart. Like the Laws of Moses were written on tablets, God wants to write his laws on our hearts. Our heart is the table where God's presence wants to dwell. He wants to live within our heart.

In the dream, the word is that the table is taken by a regular. A 'regular' is someone who comes into a place to dine on a regular basis. That person often goes to the same table and expects that it will be reserved for him because he has been there so often. He does not own the table, but has taken up ownership.

In our lives, we have allowed 'regulars' to take up ownership in the table of our hearts. We have allowed then to come and dine with us. They have given us their 'words' and we have fed on them. They have provided us with direction and teaching. We are used to them 'writing' on the tablets of our heart, so that we have not saved a place for God, when he shows up. Then when he shows up, there is no place for him.

The problem is that if we have already established our own programs, then, we do not need to hear from him on what he wants to do in our lives. If we are already on a 'reading program' that is set by some one else, then, we will reject his Holy Spirit to direct us to other portions of Scripture. If we are 'already set' in our ways, then we have filled the table and there is no place for him at our table. Often, our prayer services and worship services are 'set' and we have not saved a place for him. We have no room for him when he shows up. And he owns the place.

Truth to Show

With a humble heart I seek You Lord heart of flesh is Your reward given closed and opened by You This heart of God has turned blue with desire, load and lack Heavy laden over time with no slack pulled and pushed, taunt as a thread a heart of God can now be read for a book that is closed looks good on a stand but a book that is open can be held in Your hand grasped and learned, coddled and yearned teaching to know, truth to show.

Open Eyes

The eyes of the Lord move to and fro across the earth looking for eyes that are open. Open hearts, open eyes that He can Talk to face to face, heart to heart, to share with others, Himself.

Red Cherries

The children climb onto the old car to pick cherries
off of the big cherry tree.
They don't have a ladder, so the car works just like
one, only it holds all of them instead of only one
at a time. Why are they there? They have
been sent. But, why are they there?
They are having fun together
picking of the sweetness
for the one that they love
atop
the
family
vehicle.
We should have
fun together. We are His
children working together. It is to be one
sweet time after another for the one we love, Our Father.

Forward Window

In the car we all face the same direction. In Church,
why do we look at one another for direction? Look out the forward
window down the path that is yours.

Unified Diversity

Parquet squares in the entry way.
Diverse grains.
Unified diversity at the entrance to a house.
We walk on them, when we should walk in them.

Staple Gun

The gun isn't for shooting, but
stapling. It's not a weapon to use on one
another, but a staple gun. A staple gun only works,
when it is open. Our openness will prevail to prevent
prejudice. The ammunition God
gives us is not to shoot
people, or their
programs down,
but tack them up.
Like, on a bulletin board.
We don't tear down any one else's announcement.
We are to build up others, not discourage them.
Remember, they serve God, not us.

Just Believing

Just believing is too hard for many. We need to be careful not to judge others. They need to believe in Christ alone and Him crucified, but it is not easy. They would Do things differently if they believed.

God's Eager Power

We are conscripted to accomplish a job we never planned on. Usually, we train for a field, then scan the newspapers for a job. Not so with God's job force. We are given the title since eternity past. We are tagged in the planning room of wisdom as Her and Jesus poured over the plans for the universe, one by one they placed each person, each event, each job with just the right person. Set them in place, ready to be moved. Like horses on the starting line, they sit. Their nostrils flare and mist spews out of each side as they paw the ground. Why don't we feel the same enthusiasm? The power of God paws at the gate ready to be released within our lives by obedience to the job He has given to us. To think all that planning just might never be fulfilled by one word we say. No.

We Act Like Jesus

Your Holiness
 exceeds our expectation of who you are, O God!
Why should we be surprised
when your Holy Spirit lives within us and makes us to
become more than we have ever thought possible.
O to dream His dream!
Be His vision! Be His feet, His hands, His mouth!
To walk His walk, talk His talk!

Binding Bond of Prayer

When we pray with someone there is an eternal bond formed between us. No matter if we do not see the goal of the prayer, the first one is already answered when He binds your two souls to His, then and there.

Other's Jobs

Everybody is worried about the other job.
Let the person for it, to come and
do it. It's not even
your job to
worry about
the ones not being done.
We need to get our
own tree going.
It all comes
from your
tree. It is fruit that falls
from your tree to others when
they move you or you are moved. Shaken.

Let Him Conduct the Song

Breathe. In through the nose. Out through the mouth. Relax Leave the conductor in charge. He has the total presentation of the song in mind when He trains us to play our instrument. Just like a train conductor needs to organize the passengers into specific cars, we need to cooperate to go where He tells us to. We can't all ride in the same car. And, very rarely, the conductor will wake up one who sleeps beyond the stop. The, an amazing thing happens. The train which has already left the station, goes back to let one off at their stop. Imagine that? I did not Know that they would do that for only one person. I Guess The train is for them all, individually.

Compassion for Lost Children

The Dream: *(Paul's dream used by permission)*
There is a six year old driving an empty bus. The bus was enormous for her and the steering wheel was huge. It was a yellow school bus with green seats. She stops the bus in front of Paul and the doors open. He asks her what she is doing. She responds that She is looking for her mom. She said that her mom is dead and was a bus driver.
He responds, " Do you want me to help you find your mother?"
She says, "Yes."
So He climbs into the empty bus and the drive up and down the streets looking for her mother. They zig and zag down the streets looking for her mother. She is happy not to do it alone anymore.

Interpretation:
The child was physically, mentally and emotionally overwhelming to her. Paul showed compassion by helping her. She was looking for things that were out of her reach, including bringing her mother back to life.

In the dream, he provides her with compassion comfort, and leadership. He drives the bus demonstrating how nice he is. But, there is a problem. Paul exercises compassion, within the Child's viewpoint. They still continue to look for the dead mother. He lets her decide which direction they need to go.

The child represents a motherless child in need. She had no resources to meet her needs. She has faith in something that has died. She is using up room for the living on seeking the dead. Notice that the school bus is empty. She is seeking her mother, even though she is aware of the mother's death. Paul gets on her bus. He reaches out with compassion, comfort and meets what she says is her need. The problem is that he continues to feed into her lie. She chases a false vision and he joins in with it. She is relying on things that are dead to help her figure out things now.

Sometimes, we like the child in the dream we look for the things that are dead, that we have put away from us when we sought Christ, and try to incorporate them into our walk now. God has called us to seek Him in the land of the living.

There is a parallel between the child and Paul with regard to works and faith. The child believes that she can find the mother, even though she knows that the mother is dead. She moves on the belief that is wrong. She has no resources and is sure to be met with defeat. Paul, on the other hand, sees the child crying and in a bad situation out of her control and he enters the door, steps up to the driver's seat and assumes control where she has lost control. He exercises his faith with a demonstration of his works in action.

The only problem is that he enters into her vision and does not set her vision straight. They will both surely end in defeat. His faith has been wavered by the child because the compassion has overwhelmed his reasoning.

Job 32:18, Isa 8:18-22, II Cor 5:12-16, 9:12, James 2:22.

Compelled to Gripe

Be careful.
Don't stand around griping about others
who are trying to do God's work.
Remember that they don't work for us, but God.
If you feel compelled to gripe,
drive around the corner and wait.
God will reveal His ultimate purpose
within their life.
Your wait is on God, not on others.

Premature Gift Delivery

Sometimes in our excitement we share ourselves prematurely with others. When we share our gift with someone before it is finished, Then, often he won't understand it. It's an unfinished book, an under baked cake, the centers of a box of chocolates. Unless someone is running along the same track as you, He will not be able to see things from your perspective. Pray for God to provide a few people in your life who will understand.

Outlets

We don't need to look for ways to use our gifts. God will provide the outlets. For they are to praise Him, then it's His deal anyway.
His intake,
His outflow,
His provision,
His way,
in His time.
His deal, through us.

Overwhelming Diamond

Hook it up, connect your gift to Me,
then wait until the right time to overwhelm them
with the Spirit. My word is weighty like a rock.
It's not a paper weight, but a diamond to be put on.
Not to be admired, but worn.

Toffee

Over and above, the sweetness overflows. The candy overflows on
the dish on the table. When we are in the presence of God, with the
gifts He has given, we will overflow with His sweetness. Then, He
stretches us. And, sometimes, we feel just like toffee. Toffee
has a certain texture, chewy sweet flavor, that is not
attained by any other way. It is rolled, stretched,
twisted, and kneaded by the hand of the baker.
If we feel like we have been stretched,
it is because He wants us to have
a texture of His sweetness.
Then, when he gives the
wrappers, we will
be ready to serve
others in just
the right
way,
He
intended.
When we
Bring Jesus to
the Children,
We bring
His
sweetness,
covered with
the colorful wrapping
that He has given to us, alone.
Our individual, colorful, wrapper. Our
personality, decorated with His grace. The result
is like toffee. Toffee is tender candy, that can be given to
those without teeth, to chew. It melts in our mouth, yet has a special
texture. Tenderness abounds when His love surrounds. Bounty abounds
through hands that are willing to let go of things that keep us from
the place He wants to take us. Wrapped up in Him only.

The walk: Three Bedrooms

The Dream:
We were in a house. There were 3 bedrooms. All 3 daughters were together, so I let them decide which bed to sleep in. (My daughters, Steph, Esther, and me)

Esther chose the large double bed. It was big, but there was a corner missing. She put the games away. Stephanie has twins.

I went to the master suite. The sheer white curtains danced with the breeze from the large open windows that overlooked the rose garden.

Words:
It's not about sharing your faith with others, its about the walk.

Interpretation:
There are three ways of looking at intimacy with God. The Bed that is a double bed is a walk that cuts corners. The individual plays games with God. She has fooled herself that she is being intimate with God, but she is really playing high level games. There is not enough room in her bed for a second person; God. She likes to think that there is enough, room, but if you pull back the covers, the truth will be disclosed. She plays with God like it is a game. She cuts corners off of what God has for her. She doesn't treat sharing Christ with others seriously. She may only be trying to get numbers to 'win' the game. "The one with the most souls on their card in the end wins." These individuals are those who raise themselves above those who need saving.

The bedroom with the twin beds: This person invites God into their world then tries to reproduce themselves after him. Then they try to reproduce themselves after others and have them reproduce after them. It is spiritual cloning. God says it is not the best plan for saving souls. When we reflect God, it doesn't mean that we are a clone of him. We maintain individualistic characteristics, but we have spiritual qualities that allow us to have companionship with him in all ways.

In the third bedroom the daughter sleeps with the King. She chooses the Master suite. In this type of relationship, He cares for our his daughter. There is a 'tending' like a husband.

When we allow God to tend us like a gardener tends his plants, then he will tell us every step of the way. Then, as we do what we are supposed to do, others will notice our walk and ask us about it. This will be a constant witness to all those around us. When we focus on our intimacy with him, he will move us into position to share with others as a process of our walk. He wants to become our 'husband' and put us up in a place of resting with Him. He wants us to abide with him at his house. To enjoy His company, to become our ever present companion day and night.

Wrapped

The desires of My heart
are for you, Child
of my womb. The desire
of My soul is to
love you, have, hold,
take, envelope,
to wrap you in My
blanket from birth
and hold you close to My
chest. Be still, be wrapped.

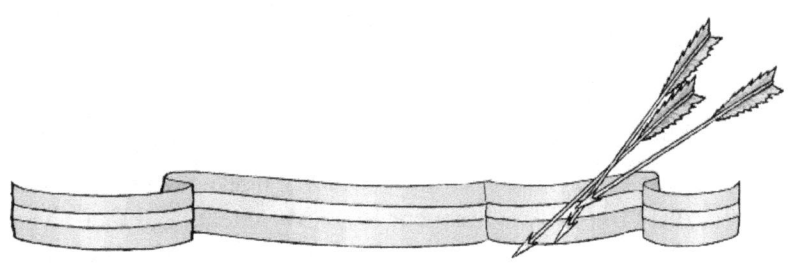

Chapter 7
Seal of Zeal

River of Light

The service of light isn't by our own hand, but through it Him to us. Love flows from a heart that is willing and able. Willing, through our will. Able through his. Joy flows. Heart released. There was a dam. There still is. But the water is so much that it overflows the dam and overflows to make pools along the river. I bring peace to get un-bound on the river.

Birthday Envelope

You tuck money in an envelope for a birthday present. I've tucked you into Me, for yours. Delight, O daughter! Your Jesus is alive and He will never tucker of tucking you into Himself. Live the love, for the love is alive. Be enveloped by Me. I need your hands, your vision, your feet. Clock in with the eternal time card and stay overtime. I will give time and a half. Just in time for mercy and grace, peace and love.

Over and above, around and thru. I love you, too. Delight, determine, deliver. He Determines to delight in us, to deliver Himself, to others.

Cuddled

Let me hold you, rock you and cuddle you like a new grandmother with a fresh family face. Wrap you, blanket you in My love. Swaddled by My hands Close to My chest Your ear to My heart. Listen! It beats a rhythm known only by those whose ear is on My chest held there by My hands, swaddled in My love, cuddled by My care, rocked in My chair.

Stick like S'mores

Unity and cohesion. Come together and stick like S'mores. We are the bound by the sweetness of God between two covenants. One, He came, he forgave. The other: He will meet us again. In between, is His sweetness where He binds us within His love which provides the cohesion for the caps.For, we are bound by grace and mercy at both sides. Eternity past, His provision. Eternity future, His provision. Forgiveness provided through Jesus. Yet, judgment taken for us in the future. We are bound between the covenants made to Abraham, and those to Jesus. In these, we become a nation, and a Kingdom. In between we are the Church. Substantiated by His grace and Mercy, we live through faith. Just like Abraham, we trust in the Covenants. And just like Jesus, we wait for them to be fulfilled. The unity and cohesion are separate issues. There can be a group of people in a stadium, Yet they root for different teams. We need to not, only have unity, but cohesion between our brethren. For, we are all bound to the same covenant. His covenant of love.
And, like S'mores, we need to stick together.

Salvation Addict

Who lives for Who? Sometimes it is hard to tell.
He loves me so much it is as if He lives to show
that love to me alone. That's how I feel. But, yet
I live for Him. To see one more person come alive
through new birth; to be born again. I am an addict.
I am like a man on a golf course. Each time I tee
off, I try to get the ball into the cup with fewer
strokes. Oh, to pray with quicker and quicker
victory for the lost to be found, sooner and
sooner, with less words. Oh, that I could
become par where I match up the with
the course God has set for me. Less
physical effort with more skill.
That I could learn the course
and play with my eyes closed
just seeing with my heart
the goals of God to be able to
visualize where they have place the flag today.
They move the flags, you know? Just like when people
come to us with needs. Each one is different. The goal
is the same; get to the cup with the least effort in the
shortest time. But, the flag has been placed a little
to one side or the other. Or, maybe, just
beyond
the horizon of our present vision. Just
because we can't see it, doesn't mean
that we don't tee off in the direction
we know the flag to be. The goal
doesn't change, and the
green will still be waiting
on the other
side of the ridge.
We stand firm, pick
up our iron, keep our vision
on Him, and take our best shot in
the direction that we know the green is.
That is why they call it an exercise of faith.

Commemorative Medals

Commemorative medals signify great events. They are stamped impressions embedded in precious elements of gold and silver. The Holy Spirit stamps His impressions on our heart, more precious than gold or silver. He embeds His ideas on us. Oh, that we may become one of God's commemorative medals for Him to proudly display.

Bursting Goodness

The popcorn bursts to life. It loves to be heated and stirred. The fire of God will come to us and burst forth with His goodness. Just like Kettle corn. It's sweet seeds become edible when the Holy Spirit stirs our heart. Seed, Oil, heat, salt, stirring. This is His special project for us. We become his light to others. He stirs by us.

Unrestrained Tenderness

Socially eloquent, intuitively astute, beautiful is your face with tears on it as you praise Me. A heart touched because you love Me. I see those tears. I count the sodium in the salt that flows down your face. Believe Me, I notice. Believe, you Me, so do they. A hungry heart in love with her Lord doesn't come their way, too often. It's moving. Unrestrained tenderness is from Me. It's Mine. You learned it from Me. A good student learns from her instructor. His tenderness abounds within His bounds.

A Burning Bush

We are a bush that burns but is not consumed; only for those around us to witness the awesome power of God.

Fruit and Light

We go to the light. A tree does not grow very well in the dark. For, it will not produce any fruit. We need fruit. A cherry tree without cherries is no good because you can't have cherry pie, cobbler, or jelly. There will be crust without filling .Topping without baked in goodness. Bread without spread. The cherry tree needs to be grown in the nursery under the supervision of the gardener.
With His grow lights.
He will care for the tender orchard bush, give it weed
and feed, trim it back when needed, and watch
with attentiveness for the first blossoms.
Because,
blossoms are a sign that fruit will follow.
When we want fruit in our spiritual life,
We need to go the nursery, get under
the light,
and let the
husband tend us.
For, He is faithful.
He will plant the seeds
of righteousness, shadow
us with Himself, and put us in
the right spot for maximum growth.
You know it will be in the full sunlight.
For, a tree grows best in the light of the sun.
We, Like cherry trees, need the Son of
God to light our way.
He will fill us, feed us, and tend our souls.
Hovering over us like an attentive gardener.
He looks for the fruit of His righteousness.
For, in the fruit are the seeds which
are planted in the fertile soil to
grow a tree that can be
put in the light.

Release of the Hearts to Sing

The further you are from the flow of the river, the further you are from that which gives life to the body of Christ. That which could not sing before has been in the cage. It is now released so it can sing. Sing and Dance of My Words into your heart. Hearts singing. The church is crying out and God has given to her. It is not what she was asking for because she only would have settled for crumbs. He Has given a feast. Life thru the Snow

Tag with Jesus

Give me your hand. Let me lead you. Forever true, never
fake, hand in hand. To the wall and touch it. Relay. Hand
off. Be a reliable relay. Pass it off. It's a tag. The play
ground is for the kids. Why? Let's play. Blow up the
size. Enlarge the fun. I want to have fun with the
kids, too. When you come to My wall,
touch Me and pass My presence
on, it will be like a playground.
It is My playground. A
place where we can
enjoy one another.
What is a playground for?
Run, Jump, slide, climb, swing, dance, twirl.
Delight in friendship, cooperation in unity, expenditure
of energy, a pull out of the regimented structure of a class
room. A break in organized learning, yet, an invaluable
time of learning to play nice. Come to My playground.
I Will teach you how to interact with others.
It will be a time of fun.
Almost like playing
games as a child.
No individual claims
the spot light; I am the
winner, all are involved,
there is activity, And My power is
expended through the body of the Church.

Custom House

Birds need a place to sing.
We've given away the bird houses
to the other
one and he has locked
it from us for the season.
Jesus is the key to rush the season.
Open the storage shed
and get back what
he stole from us.
'Thank you for making us a
custom bird house'
Sing O people!
The Lord has taken your bonds!
Sing.
Your Redeemer lives!

I Gave my Jesus Away

I gave my Bible away today. I brought a friend to Church, with the intention of showing her my Jesus. And I did. For, in the middle of worship, a gentle voice came to me and He told me to give my Bible to her. And, I loved that Bible, my husband had given it to me for my birthday. A nice maroon leather bound Bible. It had all my special scriptures marked. I only mark those I have memorized. And a testimony of an encounter with Him, on the back cover was etched in pencil.

I loved that Bible.

Isaiah was well worn, with some discoloration along the page margins Where I had turned the pages over and over in my hand. For, I love Isaiah, and Deuteronomy, and Romans, and John, and Revelation, and Hebrews, and Psalms, and Song of Solomon.

But, I could not put that voice behind me. He kept after me, telling me to give that Bible away. I had other ones. But, this was my special one. Like when my children were small, they each became attached to a blanket. They would carry it with them everywhere they went, And when I would beg to wash it, they would put a small stool in front of the washer waiting for it to come out. Then, they would gripe, because it didn't smell the same after it came out of the washer.

I am like that with my Bible. It is my blankie. Every time I am separated from it, I become stressed. I can tell you exactly where it is, because I know where I left it. It wasn't long ago, I left it. But, now the writer of the book was asking me to part from it.

So, amidst praise, I cried, and asked Him, "why, Lord?"

You know what He said? "You love it too much. I am not a book, I am a person. You love the book too much. Your relationship is not to be with a book. Give it away."

So, I did. And I have learned something. My relationship is with a person, not a book.

And, my friend; She is starting with the book, which she knows I love. She started with the well worn places, went to the verses I memorized, then read the testimony on the back cover. And, now she knows that He's more than a book. For, she didn't have a Bible like that, and now she does.

PILLOW TALK INDEX

A Burning Bush	141
Ability	23
Asleep all my Life	26
Beautiful Bloomers	112
Become Empty	73
Bequeathed	70
Bible and the Word	81
Binding Bond of Prayer	130
Birthday Envelope	137
Bubble Gum	36
Buffalo Nickle	24
Building Ourselves	109
Building the Church	80
Bursting Goodness	140
Buying Righteousness	105
By Pass of the Father	89
Can I have an Aaron?	110
Challenge	96
Check in Closet	83
Child Like Push Pins	40
Children Deserted Dad	27
Climb the Mountain	99
Commemorative Medals	140
Compassion for...Children	131
Complicate Simplicity	23
Computation	35
Conception Conversation	60
Confirmation Bridge	30
Conformation on the Bridge	29
Compelled to Gripe	132
Contemplation of Beyond	46
Coordinated Victory	23
Cracking Walnuts	115
Cuddled	138
Custom House	144
Dance with My Love	71
Dependency	98
Despite it All	24
Dream Caché	9
Driving Agony	30
Eating Like a Lamb	60
Etched in Stone	125
Everything Else	25
Faces of God	106
Feel the Power	107
Fill Your Wagon	72
Fires of Passion...Bitterness	31
Flow to Others	62
Forgiveness Slide of Jesus	84
Forward Window	128
Foundation of God's House	41
Foundation of Large Buildings	45
Free Credit	58
Fresh Oil	28
Fruit and Light	142
Geronimo	20
Glowing Embers	98
God's Eager Power	129
Gold Dust	117
God's Heart Flutter	91
God's High School Tests	95
God's Transportation System	99
Grafting into Israel	77
Half a Bridge	118
Healing Seven Ways	61
His Faithful Page	90
His Fish School	84

His Front Doors	24
His Son	20
Holiness	69
Hummers	92
Hungry	15
I Gave my Jesus Away	145
Impatient Call	123
Imprint	101
Invitation	126
Jesus Breaks the Seal	26
Jesus Fanatic Diet	15
Jesus Is	13
Joy Flows	71
Just Believing	129
Lamb's Wool Sweater	59
Laying Gold on our Paths	33
Let Him Conduct the Song	130
Let Him Push	99
Let's Be Mine	97
Light Knowledge	34
Look with God	70
Love Note	12
Love of the Father	13
Love to a Little Girl	18
Love Volley	67
Mary Anoints ...is Anointed	74
Meet at the Altar	14
Mirrors of Praise	71
Move to a New Lot	37
My Lights	71
Neglectant Drama	39
Neon Freeway Sign	98
No War in Prayer	25
Old Fashioned Time ...	59

Old Instruments of Computation	108
Open Book Life	97
Open Book Test	95
Open Eyes	127
Order of God	102
Other's Jobs	130
Our Stand	25
Outlets	133
Over and Above	37
Overwhelming Diamond	133
Pajama Party	39
Pass the Shuttle	100
Peeping Toms	114
Passwich Sandwich	88
Picking Your Fruit	47
Premature Gift Delivery	133
Prophecy Clause	114
Prudence at the Table	61
Prune to Bloom	48
Rain Water in a Cup	123
Red Cherries	127
Redemption Letters	13
Relationship with Jesus	79
Release of the Hearts to Sing	143
River of Light	137
Royalties	45
Sacrifice and Atonement	76
Salvation Addict	139
Savior Parfait	14
Savior Speaks in Dreams	38
Service Season	120
Seven Heart Tones of God	16

Seven Spirits of God	49
Shadows	93
Share	74
Spin Out	112
Shop His Movie Mall	58
Sold out to Jesus	35
Soul Checker	82
Soul Cry	32
Staple Gun	128
Stealing Uniforms	115
Stick Like S'mores	138
Store Fronts	124
Stories by Dad	44
Summer Snow	26
Sweet Jesus	76
Tag with Jesus	143
The Child Within	39
The Conquesta	11
The Dam Broke	17
The Match	69
The Oil Lamp	51
The Riches ... Released	67
The Rescue ... Through	64
The Spirit of Counsel	53
The Spirit of Might	61
The Spirit of Might Flows	119
The Steps	21
The Walk: Three Bedrooms	135
The Wounds of Jesus	65
Three Companies	90
Three Fold Wrap	104
Three Scoops of Love	14
Toffee	134
Topeka Kansas	94
Tremendous Fellowship	88
Truth to Show	127
True Purpose	112
Two AM Conversation	90
Two Arm Rescue	19
Unified Diversity	128
Unleash our Mold	75
Unrestrained Tenderness	141
Uphold Truth	125
Waiting on God	100
Washing ... Words of God	78
We Act Like Jesus	129
We are a Picture Puzzle	125
White Gloves	12
Wisdom of Proverbs	52
Who am I?	94
Why We Tremble	68
Wisdom is Found	52
Wrapped	136
Zeal	30

About the Author

Sheri Hauser grew up in Seattle, Washington accustomed to the rainy days and nights going on long hikes in the Cascades in the summer and snow skiing in the winter. She graduated from High School in Leavenworth, Washington and attended Bible College in Oregon. Married at 20, she went on to nursing school and had two children. In 2001, she began writing spiritual books and started to look for a publisher. Not finding one who would accept her manuscript, she opted to learn what was needed to grow her own publishing company. Initially the company was called Glory Bound Books and obtained license in Las Vegas in 2005. As the company grew, she tossed her entire nursing paycheck into purchasing printers and software. She attended classes at the University of Las Vegas for graphic design, web site development and photo shop. It took three years of intensive study to learn papers, the publishing industry and how to put books together. Throughout this time, she developed the Lasertrain (a set of digital templates for making your own books). She climbed the ladder of her profession and after 30 years as a Cardiothoracic Nurse in Intensive Care, she retired from nursing full-time to dedicate her time to grow a publishing company. By 2016, she had written 25 books, and published over 600 books (from authors).

Her and her husband relocated to Camp Verde, Arizona in 2017 and set the publishing company in an old house living in the upstairs. They love the quiet cowboy town and she is presently active in forming a newly developing Chamber of

Commerce. She is the president.

Additionally, she is part of the Curriculum Development Team and a Facilitator teaching classes related to publishing at Osher Life Long Learning Institute in Sedona, Clarkdale and Camp Verde.

2020 started off with a bang when she began doing ads on Amazon for her books. Today, she has 15 books on page 1 of their topic search engines and is actively seeing sales daily.

Sheri Hauser is the author of several series of books including: Glorybound Lasertrain, Dream Books with Steps to Intimacy with God, GBK Children's books and text books on publishing.

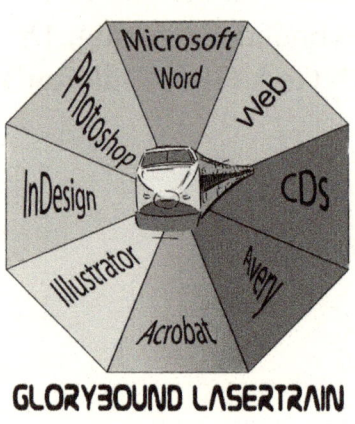

Sheri's Books

The manuals are books which help prepare for the release of the prophetic wave of the Holy Spirit as spoken of in Joel 2. These books are written from dreams. The dreams were given over a period of around 6 months or so. As they were received, I carefully interpreted them using Scriptures. Then I was given an outline dream. The dreams of the specific subject were then put into the outline. That forms the books. There are 21 books. Initially, all of the books were as one giant book. Then as I received more dreams of direction, the books began to split; first into four, then into more (like bread rising in a bowl) they grew over time within the right environment. The first book split into what became the first four books. I was instructed to turn over the stack and release them. So, I released Coriantá, having it professionally edited and printed at the cost of $37,000. By the time I got to the next book, I realized that the books were reproducing at an alarming rate, and I would never have enough money to print them conventionally, so I asked God if I could have a publishing company.

He said, "Sure."

I quickly responded, "I don't know anything about a publishing company."

His response, "That's OK. It will come in a box with instructions."

I quickly called the guy who put together my first book and then ordered the computer program which he specified as the one for making books. Guess what? It came in a box with instructions. (Smile). Several of the books sprouted due to the response from individuals asking questions-- such as *Simple Fun Christian Dream Interpretation*, the three books in the Prophetic Prayer Series as well as *Prophetic Interpretation of Art*.

All of the books are available as e-books and bound copies regular and large print through Amazon.com. Printed bound, signed, color editions are available directly through Glorybound Publishing. Use the contact page on the web site to order.

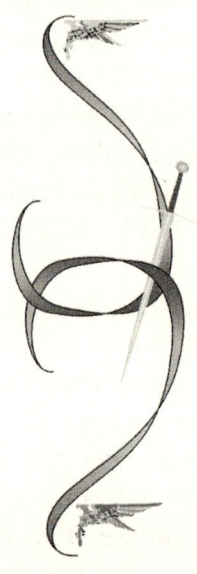

The Prophetic Wave

Manuals for a Prophetic Wave of the Holy Spirit with Miracles, Signs and Wonders

And Afterwards I will Pour Out My Spirit
Christian Authors Driving the Market
Dream Language Understood
Faith on a Wing and a Prayer
Filled with the Holy Spirit
Foundational Prophetic Prayer
Going to the Center of God's Heart
Growing Ministry to Seed instead of Fruit
Inspirational 3-D Poetry
Intimate Relationship with Jesus
Leading Prophetic Prayer
Living in the Haunted House of my Head
Living in the Shadow of the Sins of our Parents
Personal Prophetic Prayer
Preparing the Bride of Christ: Allegorical
Prophetic Interpretation of Art
Sharing Prophetic Gifts in the Church
Simple Fun Christian Dream Interpretation
Spiritual Authority Over Demon Dragons
Tactical Demonic Warfare
Why the Glory Departed

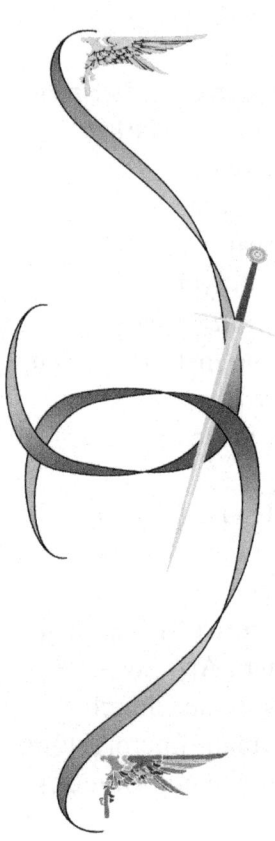

Made in the USA
Monee, IL
25 January 2021